one drum

Douglas & McIntyre

# one drum

## Stories and Ceremonies for a Planet

# RICHARD WAGAMESE

2 3 4 5 6 — 23 22 21 20 19

Douglas and McIntyre (2013) Ltd.
P.O. Box 219, Madeira Park, BC, V0N 2H0
www.douglas-mcintyre.com

Epigraph, page 7, excerpted from "Grandfather Look at Our Brokenness,"
from *Songs for the People* by Art Solomon (NC Press Ltd., 1990) reprinted with
the permission of Eva Solomon.

Cover design by Anna Comfort O'Keeffe
Text design by Diane Robertson

Printed and bound in Canada

Douglas and McIntyre (2013) Ltd. acknowledges the support of the Canada
Council for the Arts, which last year invested $153 million to bring the arts to
Canadians throughout the country.

*Nous remercions le Conseil des arts du Canada de son soutien. L'an dernier, le
Conseil a investi 153 millions de dollars pour mettre de l'art dans la vie des Cana-
diennes et des Canadiens de tout le pays.*

We also gratefully acknowledge financial support from the Government
of Canada and from the Province of British Columbia through the BC Arts
Council and the Book Publishing Tax Credit.

Library and Archives Canada Cataloguing in Publication

Title: One drum : stories and ceremonies for a planet / Richard Wagamese.
Names: Wagamese, Richard, author.
Identifiers: Canadiana (print) 20190159952 | Canadiana (ebook) 20190160179
| ISBN 9781771622295
  (softcover) | ISBN 9781771622301 (HTML)
Subjects: LCSH: Rites and ceremonies—Canada. | LCSH: Ojibwa philosophy. |
LCSH: Healing. | CSH:
  Native peoples—Canada—Rites and ceremonies.
Classification: LCC E99.C6 W34 2019 | DDC 299.7/8333038—dc23

A NOTE FROM THE PUBLISHER: Richard Wagamese was working on this manuscript in the three years prior to his death. Regrettably, he did not have the time to fulfill his original plan to write stories and ceremonies inspired by each of the foundational teachings of the Ojibway tradition, the Seven Grandfather Teachings. Still, the manuscript has much to offer readers, and it has been published here, as the author penned it, with minimal edits. As Wagamese wrote, he was not a traditionalist but "merely one who has trudged the same path many of this human family has—the path of the seeker, called forward by a yearning I have not always understood."

In this book, Richard Wagamese gives us four small, doable ceremonies, ceremonies for people of all cultures and beliefs—and it was his hope that in following them, readers would be inspired to connect with the rest of humanity and every other living thing on the planet, and live life itself as a ceremony.

It is our hope that the reader will draw inspiration from these writings and find their own path, filling in what Wagamese did not have the chance to put down on paper. For as he wrote in these pages, "Within each of us is a shaman. Within each of us is a teacher. Within each of us is a storyteller. These are powerful roles that are vital to our collective survival."

And as Wagamese also wrote, a ceremony is not complete until it is shared. In keeping with that idea, it seems fitting that here is his final manuscript, shared.

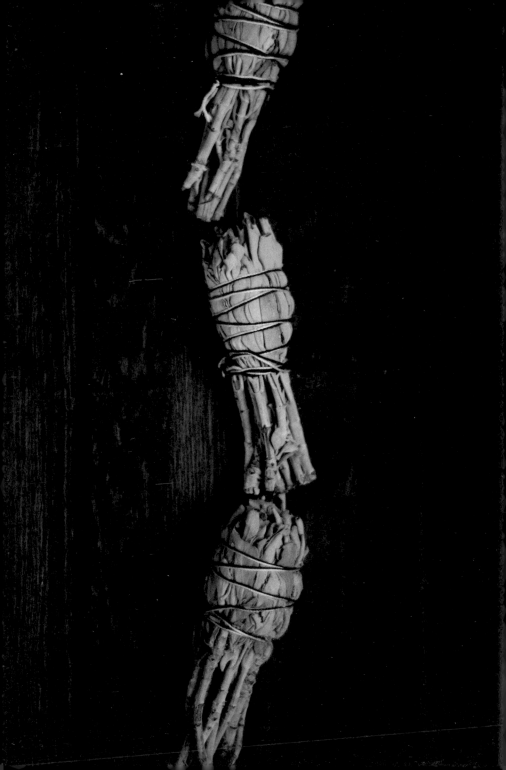

Grandfather
Look at
Our brokenness.
[...]
We know that we are the ones
Who are divided
And we are the ones
Who must come back,
Together,
To worship and walk
In a sacred way,
That by
Our Affirmation,
We must heal the earth
And heal each other.

—from *Songs for the People*,
Art Solomon, Ojibway Elder

# contents

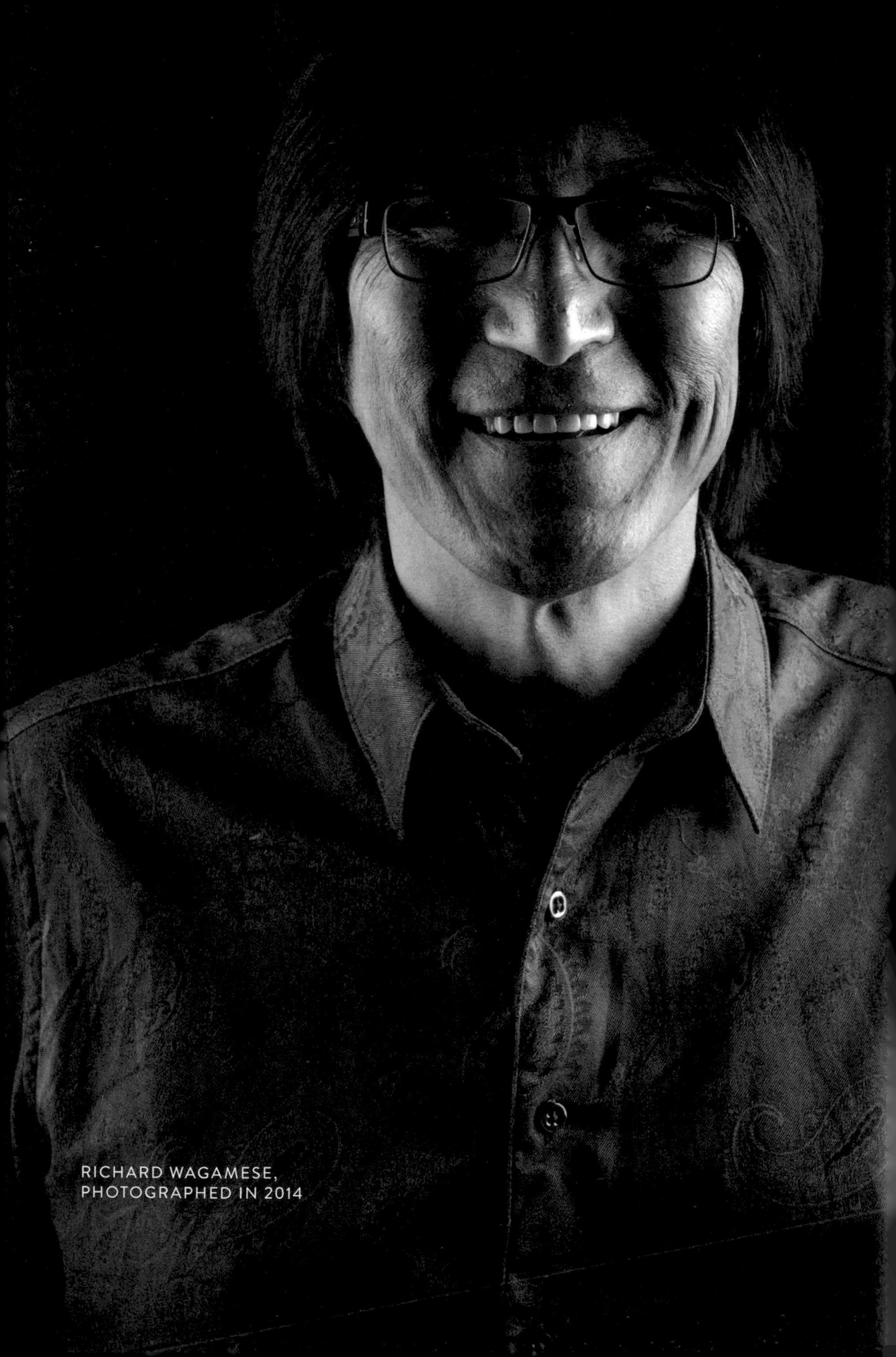

RICHARD WAGAMESE,
PHOTOGRAPHED IN 2014

# foreword

WHEN I THINK of seminal writers who have taken it upon themselves to document the journey of Canada's Indigenous people and had the ability to change society's impression, only a handful come to mind, including Tomson Highway, Lee Maracle, Thomas King and, of course, Richard Wagamese.

Richard and I were friends. Not best friends, as he lived on the other side of the country and had interests that differed from mine, but we would still greet each other warmly when a literary festival or conference would put us in the same hotel. Once when on a trip into my territory, he and his partner stopped in at my reserve for a visit. I managed to convince them to break their cleanse and enjoy some organic, cruelty-free sausages I was barbecuing. I felt oddly delighted at that slight act of corruption. Oh, and if you want to hear a funny story about Richard's underwear and then mine, feel free to ask Shelagh Rogers. I can see you smiling already.

But more importantly, I was a fan of both the man and his work. Richard had talent and a unique style. While quick to smile—and his whole face would light up when that smile chose to appear—he was perhaps known for the seriousness of his work. A survivor of cross-cultural adoption policies frequently known as the "Scoop Up," Richard was an unparalleled spokesman for those who suffer from what I call Post Contact Stress Disorder. His work, fiction and non-fiction alike, told the story of entire generations of Indigenous people who were commonly at odds with the Canadian Dream.

His mastery and control of the written language was something to envy. Though in our communities both English and print were invasive species, Richard had the talent to indigenize it to the point of giving his writing its own status card. More importantly, Richard was not just a writer, or a storyteller, he was a philosopher, though such a moniker would no doubt have made him blush. Upon reading his work, especially this new book, it occurs to me that the way he thought and strung those thoughts together, binding his own personal experiences with those of our Elders' teachings, could only come from a mind that had lived a life like his. Good and bad journeys, mixing in the mind that created the literary legacy that includes *Starlight, Embers, Indian Horse* and this, his final collection of personal thoughts.

*One Drum* explores the Seven Grandfather Teachings, an investigation into what many Anishnawbe consider the seven fundamental truths of living a good and productive life. As is his usual style, Richard wanders through traditional teachings, bittersweet reflections, and a desire to understand how it all ties together. Unfortunately, he only managed to complete his interpretation of the first three. One can only wonder what else he would he have had to say about the rest. Alas, one of the great unanswered questions in the universe.

Still, we should be grateful that we have this last glimpse into the thoughts of Richard Wagamese. I sometimes wonder if it was musings like this that helped keep some of his monsters at bay. He had demons that haunted him, but perhaps that was what helped fuel some of his genius. I can't say. But I can say his characters were all so real and yet so literary, and always as complex as he was.

I too view the world through stories—just recently I was in Bremen, Germany, attending a small authors' festival. I managed to sneak away to see some of the city and found myself walking along a large park. Nestled not far inside, I found a nice restaurant. Realizing I was hungry, I decided to partake. The waitress, a young woman possibly on either side of twenty, asked where I was from. Upon finding out Canada, she eagerly mentioned she was taking a literary course and was currently reading a book called *Indian Horse*. I literally did a double take. She seemed so delighted that I knew not only the book but also the author, whom she greatly admired. Richard's fans were and are international.

While having their origins in Anishnawbe culture, the Teachings of the Seven Grandfathers are open to all. Richard knew that.

It was an honour and a privilege to know Richard Wagamese the writer, the friend, the man. And by reading this book, perhaps you too can catch a glimpse of the man who put these words to paper. Writing is like DNA—practically everything about a writer is there, you just have to know where and how to look for it. I leave you to that adventure.

—Drew Hayden Taylor
  Curve Lake First Nation
  June 2019

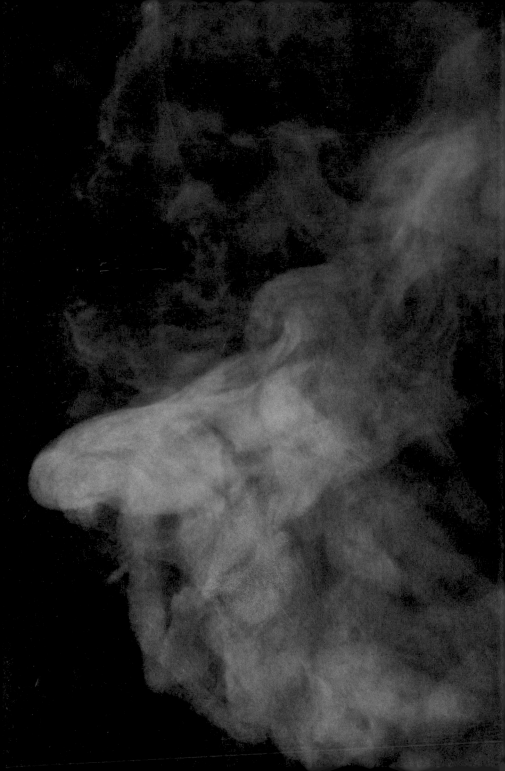

# introduction

MEDICINE BURNS WHEN touched by fire. The smoke
curls and spirals upward, plumes of it rising, swirling,
pushing themselves in ribbons higher and higher until the
smell of it becomes the ancient aroma of blessing, teaching
and communion. Within its fragrant cloud you can feel
peace descend upon you. There is Spirit here. You can feel
it if you allow it and that is the heart of the Teaching—the
Allowing. If you close your eyes and breathe, drawing both
air and blessing inside you and then exhaling long and
slow and languidly, you can come to know that Harmony
is a living thing—if you allow it. When you do, the act of
burning medicine becomes a ceremony, and in this small,
ritual way you are transformed, at once becoming more spirit
than physical self, and the blessing is the feeling that comes
over you. Emotion becomes your own medicine, rising with
the smoke, higher and higher and higher, until it reaches
that point of disappearing, vanishing, changing worlds and
bearing your thought and hope and prayer outward into the
realm of the Spirit World, where all petitions are heard. This
is spiritual. This is truth. This is Indian.

In our Native way the medicines are sweetgrass, sage, cedar
and tobacco. The smoke of them is the smudge that we pass

over ourselves to return us to the purity and innocence we were born with. It cleanses us. It soothes us. It makes us ready for the ongoing ceremony of life. To smudge is to open ourselves to receive. To smudge is to become prayerful. To smudge is to join our energy to the great wheel of nurturing, creative, loving energy that is Creation—and it is the doorway to true Consciousness. This is also spiritual. This is also truth.

But it is not ours alone.

Everywhere around the world people are engaged in ceremony. The ceremonies take many forms. They are borne outward as prayers and songs and petitions in many languages. They are partaken in geographies as diverse as the looks of our physical selves. Around the world humankind shares a deep and resonant yearning for connection with the cosmos, with spirituality, community and the planet. We're all going somewhere. We can feel that. We just don't want to make the journey alone—and we never have. In the primitive times that were our common beginning, we were wanderers. All of us. Every contemporary culture shares this origin. We followed game and other food. We foraged to survive. Every night, fires were lit and everyone gathered around them. Everyone sat and basked in the flickering light of the flames and the first thing that fire engendered in them was feeling. They felt secure from the hard dark around them. They felt safe in the company of each other. They felt belonging and worth and acceptance. They felt the mystery, the invisible energy of the universe all around them.

It was then that stories were told. The wise ones in their midst, the seers, spun great legends and teaching tales and the people learned that the world and the universe were full and alive and evolving. Out of those great tales came the feeling of mystery, of awe. Later, alone perhaps, standing outside the influence of that fire, one of our ancestors put their head back and scanned the heavens. It would have been a spectacular sight. Free of carbon clouds, the sky would shimmer brilliantly with the light of a million stars. The sense of space would be captivating. The ancestor felt wonder and out of that feeling came the need for ceremony, for rituals to re-create that feeling of wonder within their participants. And the quest for a spiritual life was born. Everywhere. In everyone. Wonder is the gift we share—if we allow it.

My people say that none of us can claim a right to a spiritual way. The word *spiritual* itself means "of the spirit." We are all spirit. We are all energy. The truth is that there is a fire that burns at the invisible centre of all of us. It is lit by the embers of those tribal fires where we used to sit and feel yearning deep within us. That yearning is another gift. It is a calling. It is our intuition. It is our most ancient voice speaking to us. When there was no language, our ancestors communicated with it. So when we learn to hear it and respond to it, intuition asks us to travel inside ourselves to sit in the warmth of that ancient and eternal flame. We all carry those embers. No matter what life throws at us, no matter the pain and suffering and abuse we may have endured, that

*wonder*
IS THE GIFT WE SHARE
*—if we allow it*

tiny flame flickers in the deepest chamber of our being. It is sacred and it is eternal. When we allow a sense of wonder to inhabit us, something magical and universal happens within us. We feel. Something "of the spirit" flickers to life in us and we feel spiritual. Within that elevated spiritual feeling we begin to believe we can transcend our difficulties and old pain. We can. We seek out ceremony to help us rekindle that sense of awe and wonder and hope. We attend ceremonies in churches, mosques, temples, meeting houses, gurdwaras, jinjas, fire temples and Kingdom Halls. We also attend them in yurts, igloos, teepees, kivas and wigwams. No one way is the definitive one. Each way is merely a path toward the fulfillment of our common dream—communion.

When my people speak of communion they do not refer to religious ceremony. Instead they refer to the act of aligning personal energy with Earth energy, universal energy and, ultimately, eternal energy. All of our rituals, from prayer to smudging to the Pipe Ceremony to the Sun Dance and the sweat lodge, are about the act of aligning energy—of allowing our spirit to enter the flow of the great circle of spiritual energy that is everywhere around us. Always.

That's the truth of it. It is inescapable. Even when we do not allow ourselves to believe it, that great truth abides: the truth that everything is energy and that everything was born within it to live within it; that there is no death, only a returning to the fold of it again to be carried on its current and borne again to life. Reborn. That is the great promise because a circle has no end—only continuation. When we smudge with our

medicines, what it means, in the Native way, is that we choose
to respond to our inherent yearning for unity and harmony
with all that is. We choose to allow peace to reside within us.
We choose to allow our energy to meld with spiritual energy
and become part of the eternal circle.

All faiths and all peoples have medicine. That is a great truth
too. Medicine refers to those things that return us to balance,
to wellness, to our proper size and, in the end, to innocence,
to the humility that is the root of all believing. Humility is
another gift we share. Perhaps it is our greatest gift, because it
is so difficult to return to and hold. There is medicine in great
books. There is medicine in ritual. Medicine resides in prayers,
petitions, songs, chants, incense, the elements of the Earth and,
most powerfully, in solitude, when we take the time to get at
ourselves and ponder, reflect and pray. In truth, we were given
this planet to walk upon so that we might find the medicines
that would return us to humility, and from there begin the
great spiritual journey to the fullest expression of ourselves.
This was not given solely to the Indigenous peoples of North
America—it was given to all of us and we have all found our
medicine ways.

We have also all forgotten them.

Humility's opposite is pride. Pride's foundation is built on
fear. The energy of fear is a circle too. There is abiding fear
among all of us that there will not be enough. That there
is judgment. That failure exists. That this life is all there is.
Every person from every culture shares these fears and out

WE HAVE
ALWAYS BEEN
*one song*

of them come a host of others, so that now, in these times, we feel farther apart from each other than ever before. Ironically, at the same time, we have developed technology that allows us to communicate faster over greater distances. What we fail to recognize is the relationship between the words *communication* and *commune*, and the spiritual word *communion*. To be in harmony.

Our world draws out our differences. Fear masked as pride allows us to create separation between us. These rifts exist in neighbourhoods, communities, towns, cities, societies and nations. They exist between countries and ideologies and most powerfully, and sadly, in our individual homes. We have learned collectively that it is easier to push away than it is to bring closer. So we allow our differences to keep us apart. The act of communion has become disempowered and our human family has returned to the state of individual bands of wanderers.

My people say that this time was foretold. Our ancient prophecies said that there would come a time when words would fly like lightning bolts across the sky. This referred to the age of satellites and the internet. These same prophecies predicted that the human family would move farther apart and that this separation, this break in energy, would cause great stress upon the Earth. This time would be marked by flood, drought, titanic storms, famine, earthquakes, the departure of the animals, strange diseases and turmoil among all peoples. One look at the news on any given day will reveal these predictions are coming true.

But my people say that there will also come a time when a new flame is lit. A new fire will burn and the human family will gather about it for shelter, warmth, community and belonging. This new flame will be ignited by the embers of those old tribal fires we have in common. There will be a returning to teachings that draw us together instead of pushing us apart. As these teachings are renewed, the human family will gather together and the energy of that joining will heal the planet—if we allow it.

That is what this book is about.

See, my people say that we are all one song. We are born of the same spiritual energy. We are created in its image and we carry it within us. As we walk upon the Earth we move with the same eternal rhythm that beats within it. The heartbeat. The Earth is a drum, a spiritual being, and the beat of it is the first sound we hear in the darkness of our mother's belly. The drum of her. The heartbeat. It comforts, consoles, nurtures and protects us as we form and as we learn to listen for that sound in the darkness. When we are born and we come out into this reality to find our identity, the first thing we do is cry. We cry at the sudden separation from that heartbeat.

Our spirit journey on the planet is to seek reunion with that heartbeat. That's why drums were the first instruments developed by cultures around the world. All of us seek a reconnection to that same eternal, spiritual heartbeat. All of us seek a reconnection to creative, nurturing spiritual energy. All of us carry that yearning, and we created ceremony and ritual and religions out of that ache. So the truth is that we have always been one song.

In our separation the song is diminished and the Earth shows the effects of that. What is needed now is a return to elemental teaching. We need to recognize the fact that we are all one song, one family, one energy and one soul. For when my people say "all my relations" at the end of a ceremony or a prayer, it is in recognition of that truth. It does not mean only those who look like me, sound like me, speak the same language as me or live like me. It means *all*, every voice in our common chorus. We need to return to that teaching now for the good of the planet we call our home. Because what swims underneath that teaching is another universal truth: that if we are all here to find the highest possible expression of ourselves, then our common journey is a spiritual one, not a political, cultural or ideological one—a spiritual one. What drives that journey is one song: a song called yearning. What drives that song is one drum ringing out from the universal heartbeat we all seek connection to.

So the most profound truth in the universe is this: we are all one drum and we need each other.

For a long time my people were reluctant to share their teachings. When the settlers arrived in North America they did not understand the nature of our drums, and consequently, our rituals, because they had set aside their own drums a long time before. They saw what we practised as flying in the face of the religion they held as true. So our rituals and ceremonies were outlawed and forced to go underground in order to survive. The result of having to practise ceremony in secret was secrecy

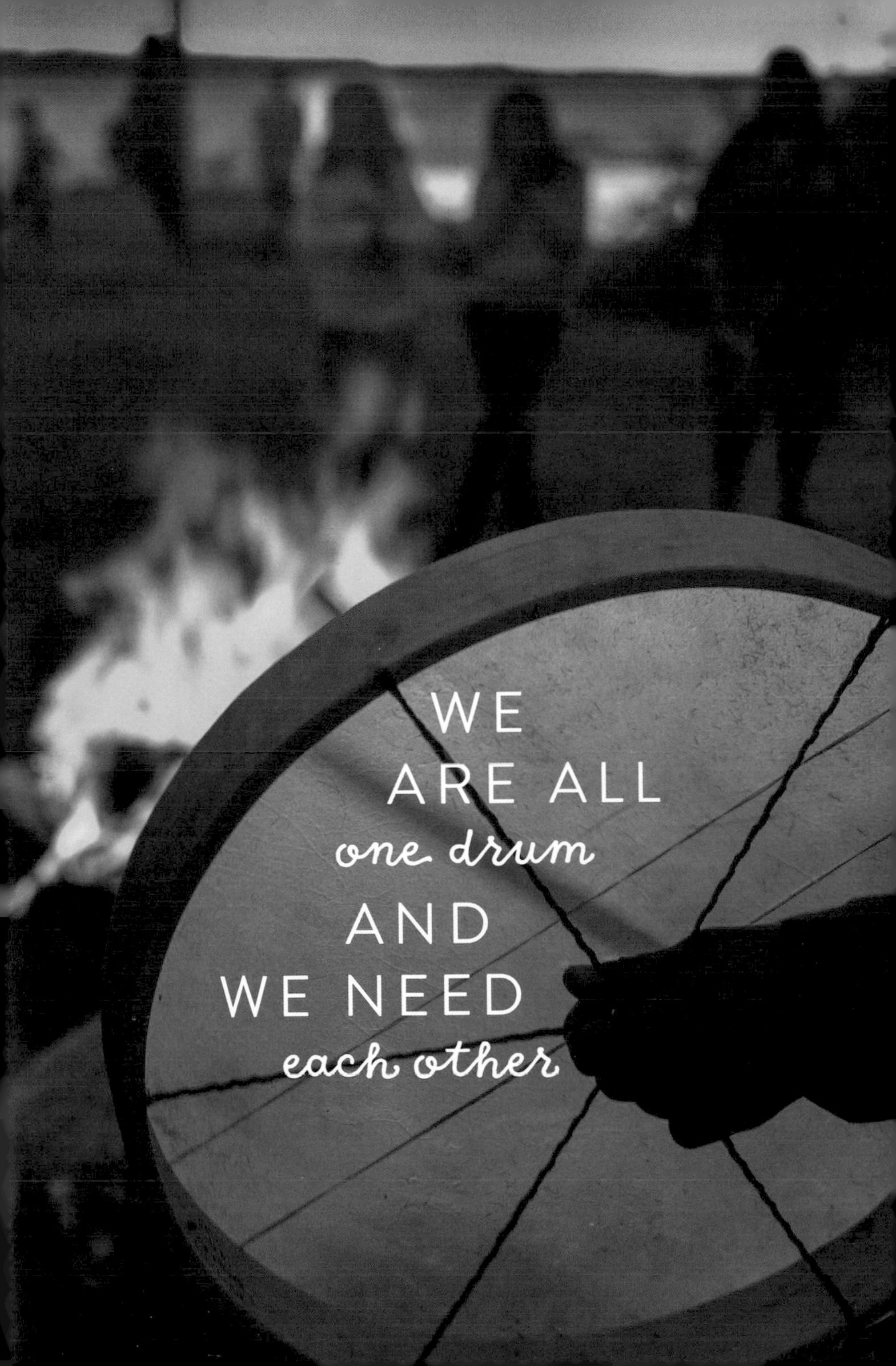
WE
ARE ALL
one drum
AND
WE NEED
each other

THERE IS A
*shaman*
IN EACH OF US
*&* WE ARE ALL
*teachers*

itself, and the fear that it would all be taken away. So for a long time Indigenous people did not share their teachings. Some even came to believe that a person had to qualify or that some did not belong. But one thing that is absolutely true is that unity and separation cannot exist in the same place at the same time. It is also true that harmony cannot coexist with exclusion. So our teachers began to welcome others into our circles, and we have welcomed many people from many cultures to ceremonies, cultural gatherings and teaching circles.

But we need to go further. As a human family we need to work deliberately at harmony. That is what the Earth requires. Harmony is the energy that heals. However, it is a sad truth of the nature of our lives that many have no access to traditional teachers or the ceremonies and teachings that sustain a spiritual way. Even among my own people this is true.

This book will draw from foundational teachings of Ojibway tradition called the Seven Grandfather Teachings to illustrate, in a contemporary way, how all of us can use universal spiritual truths to find harmony in our lives and communities. The Seven Grandfather Teachings—humility, courage, respect, love, honesty, truth and wisdom—are an ancient way of recognizing the principles required to live a good life in a good way. They incorporate all levels of our being: the physical, the emotional, the mental and the spiritual. However, I am not a shaman. Nor am I an elder, a pipe carrier or a celebrated traditionalist. I am merely one who has trudged the same path many of this human family has—the path of the seeker, called forward by a yearning I have not always understood. I have fallen many times but I have always stood up on my feet and felt urged to continue on the path. That has been my blessing because I have been fortunate to have been guided by genuine, spiritual people who gave freely of what they carried and asked only that I share it when the time was right. That time is now.

This book offers simple ceremonies that anyone anywhere can do, alone or in a group, to create harmony, re-energize the planet and bring individual energies into the great nurturing and creative circle of energy that surrounds us. There is a shaman in each of us and we are all teachers. This is what my people say. In the world of the spirit there is no right way or wrong way. These simple rituals are meant to honour the one song that we are and the one drum that guides us. When they are performed from the place of yearning we share, they are a blessing to our home, this Earth, who in our Ojibway language we call Aki.

These ceremonies are meant to function as one song. An honouring song. In our teaching way, an honour song is sung in recognition of the spirit. The more voices raised, the stronger the song reverberates, allowing it to resonate from our physical plane outward into the spiritual plane, where all the ancestors join the celebration. Such a song can bring all of our energies into line with the eternal energy. When that happens, we truly become one song and one drum beating together in a common purpose—and we are healed.

beginnings

**It begins**, as all things do, with stories. When our ancestors gathered around their tribal fires, stories were told. As a human family we have this tradition in common. Many have forgotten their beginnings, but next time you are out with people and it is a summer night and a campfire is lit, watch how everyone responds to it. As night falls and the flames climb higher, people, regardless of their cultural background, will lean in toward the flame. Some will cup their chin in their hands. Others will lean forward with their elbows on their knees. Still others might lean back in their chair and idle there, never taking their eyes off the fire. A pervasive quiet descends and soon there is only the crackle of the fire, the snap of the logs. Everyone breathes more deeply. Everyone relaxes. This scenario happens everywhere around the world when people gather in a circle around a fire in the night. I believe it is because we all carry a specific cellular memory based on the spiritual feeling of togetherness, safety and belonging. It is the basis of our human identity— community—and it formed in all of us a long, long time ago. There is a particular magic that exists when the world is reduced to a flame and the sound of a human voice talking. We all respond to that setting like children, rapt with wonder and entranced by the possibility of story.

The teachers of our cultures recognized this. They could see wonder on the faces. And so storytelling became a central tradition of the human family everywhere. What begins in wonder is learned in earnest. This is the truth those teachers gleaned from the ambience of fireside. So the truth of our interrelationship with each other, our connectedness, our family tie, is that story is our most powerful commonality—and so it begins with one.

In the Long Ago Time the world was new and fresh. The Anishinabeg (the name Ojibway people refer to themselves by) were given the Earth as their home. It was given as a place where they could learn to live a good life, known in their language as *mino-bimaadiziwin*. Their original instruction, as they went out into this reality, was to walk gently upon the Earth and do each other no harm. For many generations the people walked their new home in a state of wonder at its perfection, its beauty and its abundance.

But prior to their arrival, Creator had called the Animal People together in a great circle. Creator told them about the strange new creature that was coming to live among them. At that time there were only Animal People and they could speak to each other with one mind, with one language. They shared the planet and accepted each other and respected their differences and the attributes each of them carried, so the Earth was a place of harmony. Creator asked the Animal People to assume the responsibility of becoming the Teachers of the new beings.

"No one knows the Earth as well as you. There are no other beings who respect it so greatly or who have the vision to see it as it is—as alive and as a spiritual being. This makes you the most natural of teachers. I want you to take the responsibility of teaching the New Ones how to live upon it, how to learn from it and how to use it to find their way to the highest possible expression of themselves." This is what Creator told them.

Naturally, because they loved the Earth and because of the magnitude of Creator's request, the Animal People accepted this great honour. When the first Anishinabeg emerged from the Earth and began to walk around, the Animal People introduced themselves and became the Anishinabeg's guides and advisors according to Creator's wishes. They allowed the new beings to become their family—and a relationship was born.

With such forthright guides the human beings flourished. Whenever there was doubt or hesitancy there was always a member of the Animal People to show the way. Sometimes, animals gave up their lives to allow the new beings to live and grow, and it was in this way that Sacrifice became a spiritual principle. At that time in their history the human beings recognized Sacrifice for what it was and learned to offer prayers and to be thankful for the mercy shown by their teachers. For a long time there was peace and an overwhelming feeling of community and family upon the Earth.

But then a strange thing began to happen. Creator had told the Animal People that the new beings would differ from them in one striking way: they would come out upon the Earth not knowing who they were. Unlike the Animal People, who

*harmony*
IS THE
*energy*
THAT BINDS
ALL THINGS
*together*

were born knowing this absolutely, the human beings would arrive with no understanding of their identity. Their spiritual mission would be to come to that understanding. To help them, Creator would send them out onto the Earth bearing strange gifts that would help them discover themselves, and fulfill their destiny and their purpose.

One of these gifts was the ability to dream. With this gift the human beings would create amazing works of art, invent awesome tools and eventually come to inhabit all corners of the Earth. But each new invention would take them further and further away from their teachers. It would be hard but Creator asked the Animal People to be strong through those times and remain true to the New Ones. Because they were spiritual beings, the Animal People swore to uphold their role.

The second of these gifts was reason. Because the Animal People were born knowing exactly who and what they were, they had no use for reason; they reacted to the world spiritually. But the New Ones needed a tool to discover the importance of a spiritual way, and reason was that tool. They just did not recognize it as such. Instead, the newcomers would begin to trust the power of their minds over the power of their spirits and they would become lost and lose touch with the Earth. Again, Creator asked the Animal People to remain steadfast in their role and not abandon them. Again, they swore to remain true to their new brothers and sisters.

Many moons passed. As dreams came to them the human beings began to change. They moved away from the One

Mind the Animal People had shown them, and created their own language. With this new way of talking, the Animal People could not share their knowledge with them. The newcomers began to reason that there were ways of getting more of the bounty the Earth provided, and it was then that greed and envy were born, and the fear of lack, of not having enough. With this new development, true community was fractured and the human beings split up into separate bands.

The people began to live in the opposite of a spiritual way. They followed the lead of reason, and their ability to use the spiritual power of dreams shrank and withered. Jealousy, fear, suspicion and mistrust began to grow among the separate bands and the Animal People could not reach out to them anymore. The spiritual ones among the newcomers tried to remind them of their original instructions—to walk gently upon the Earth and to do each other no harm. But fear is the companion of reason and even though their animal guides offered their guidance, the people were too busy plotting against each other and refused to listen. They had come to reason that those who owned more held more power. Power became more vital than anything. Harmony was lost.

It was then that Creator determined to flood the Earth and begin again. But Eagle flew to Creator and asked for a favour.

"We have sworn to be their teachers and their guides," Eagle said. "There is not a one of us who does not respect that oath and seek to continue in our role. So allow me to fly around the world and find one spiritual human being to bring to you for instruction. If I cannot find such a one, then continue on this path."

Creator respected Eagle's courage and loyalty. Creator granted the favour and Eagle flew off in search of a pure heart and a pure spirit. She flew for many days. She travelled enormous distances to every place the human beings had come to reside and everywhere she saw evidence of their straying from the spiritual way. It was disheartening. But Eagle believed that there were human beings who lived according to the original instructions and even though she wearied, she continued to fly. Finally, on the shore of a sparkling blue lake, she saw a small band of Anishinabeg. As she soared over them she saw that they were still living in a spiritual manner and her heart was gladdened.

There was a young couple living there. They had a small baby boy. The young one was tucked in a cradleboard and set under the boughs of a tall pine tree. Eagle flapped down and sat in the topmost branches and watched over him. The young couple lived simply and showed great respect for the Earth and offered prayers for everything they gathered. They treated those around them gently. They shared what they had and they showered their child with spontaneous and open love. Eagle knew she had found the true spirit she had come to find.

She flew off and gathered gifts of tobacco and red cloth. When she returned she left these gifts under the pine tree so that the young couple would know that the coming event was a spiritual one and they should not fear. Then she took the cradleboard in her talons and flew back to where Creator sat with seven spiritual beings. In Ojibway they are called *Niizhwaaswi Mishomis*. Seven Grandfathers.

"I have found the one I sought," Eagle said and laid the cradleboard down at the feet of the Grandfathers.

They peered into the cradleboard where the young one slept. He was innocent and peaceful. Finally, one of the Grandfathers spoke.

"This is the one. Take him now and travel all over the Earth and teach him carefully the way the Anishinabeg should live their lives. Instruct him well and then bring him back to us."

Eagle was heartened. Gathering the cradleboard in her talons she flew off on her great mission. They travelled for seven years and the boy was introduced to the Earth in a sublime and spiritual way. Eagle took the boy to Wise Ones who taught him carefully about the use of ceremony. Through these teachings he came to understand the relationship between all things. He came to understand that ceremony is the way to direct spirituality and that spirituality is the path to harmony. He came to understand that harmony is the energy that binds all things together.

When the seven years were up, Eagle took the boy back to the Grandfathers. He was already a young man because spiritual time and Earth time move in different rhythms. The Grandfathers sat and talked with the boy for a long time. They could see that he was very honest and that he had taken all the teachings he had received to heart. One of the

HUMILITY
IS THE FOUNDATION
*of everything*

Grandfathers took a drum and began to sing. Then he took a cloth that was woven of every colour.

"This cloth represents all of the Teachings. It is yours to carry," the Grandfather said, holding it out to the young man.

"But I am not finished yet," said Eagle. "There is more for him to learn."

The Grandfathers respected Eagle's commitment and she and the boy flew off again. They travelled widely and the boy learned even more from all the Wise Ones from every band. When Eagle determined that the boy understood enough about spiritual ways to sit with the Grandfathers, they returned.

As they sat and talked with the boy, who was now a grown man, the Grandfathers were touched by his earnest respect for everything he had learned. He held the Teachings in his heart and he allowed the Great Mystery of things to remain a mystery, merely offering tremendous respect for it and not allowing himself to reason it away, alter it or reshape it to his thinking. The Grandfathers knew he was ready to carry the Teachings they wanted to bring back to the Earth.

One by one the Grandfathers offered him the Teachings he would carry to the human beings—the Teachings that would guide them to a good life. "These are the ones you take with you," he was told.

The first Grandfather offered Humility. "Humility is the foundation of everything. To know yourself as a sacred part of Creation is to know Humility."

The second Grandfather gave him Courage. "Courage is the foundation of faith. To face a foe with integrity is to have Courage."

The third Grandfather spoke of Respect. "Humility in action is Respect. To honour all of Creation is to have Respect."

The fourth Grandfather offered Love. "The energy that heals all things is Love. To know Love is to know Peace. To extend Love is to create Peace."

The fifth Grandfather spoke of Honesty. "To carry Honesty is to recognize Equality. There is none lesser or greater. To treat all as your brother or your sister is to carry Honesty."

The sixth Grandfather held out Truth. "To know all of these things is to know Truth."

The seventh Grandfather offered Wisdom. "Every earnest search arrives here. To cherish knowledge is to know Wisdom."

The boy who was now a man stood and gathered these Teachings together in a bundle. Then he and Eagle returned to the reality of the human beings. When he was back, he introduced his people to ceremonies that would lead them to each of the sacred teachings. Every ceremony and every ritual he brought gave the people the opportunity to bring their energy into the flow of nurturing, healing and creative energy that is Creation. Sometimes the people flourished and sometimes they struggled, for this is the way of a spiritual search, but with the Teachings of the Seven Grandfathers a

TO CHERISH
*knowledge*

IS TO KNOW
*wisdom*

path was cleared through the shadows of unknowing, and they began the eternal walk toward their destiny and the highest possible expression of themselves.

THIS IS THE story the way that I was given it. My people say that every Anishinabe speaks of these teachings differently. While that is true, the essence of the story remains the same— that we are given specific teachings whose sole purpose is to show us how to follow the original instructions: to walk gently upon the Earth and do each other no harm. To live a good life. The further we separate ourselves from these teachings, the more we lose our way and create disharmony. When disharmony appears, the flow of energy is disrupted, things become difficult and the path is hard to find again. Our human history shows this to be true and in these times—the times foretold—there is a desperate need for us to embrace the teachings that were meant for the whole human family.

See, *Anishinabeg* does not just mean the Ojibway. It is merely the way my people choose to refer to themselves. It translates to "the people." The spiritual salutation "All My Relations" means everybody, everywhere, in all times. It also refers to everything present in Creation. The salutation is offered as recognition that we are all one energy, one soul, one song and one drum. So the Teachings apply to everyone who struggles to find a spiritual path for themselves and for everyone who comes to love the Earth and seeks to honour her as Mother

Earth—the place of all beginnings. The Teachings exist as brought into this reality through Ojibway culture, world view, philosophy and spirituality, but they were meant as guidelines, as a way of being, for the Anishinabeg—the people.

DIBAADENDIZIWIN:
*humility*

# In the Long Ago Time when there

were only Animal People, they decided that they needed to choose a leader. They held a meeting in a great meadow and there was much sage discussion about how this would happen. All members of the animal kingdom were there: birds, reptiles, insects and all of the four-leggeds. This was in the time when the Animal People could speak to each other with one mind in one common language, so even the fish and those others that swim could be heard. It was a very solemn occasion.

"A leader must be strong and proud," said Buffalo, and the entire circle murmured at his wisdom.

"A leader must carry the medicine power of wisdom," said Wolverine, and there was much discussion about his offering.

"A leader must have a powerful presence. One that commands respect," said Wolf, and all nodded in agreement.

Around and around the discussion went. There were many admirable suggestions about the attributes of leadership but no one could come up with a process for choosing. The Animal People lived in harmony and the idea of creating a hierarchy, of elevating one over another, was beyond them. As the talk continued they became discouraged and wondered if there was a respectful and honourable way to choose a leader. The day lengthened and evening started to slide across the sky and still there was no consensus.

Then a small voice spoke. Everyone strained to hear and when the voice was located the Animal People separated and made way for the speaker to come forward and address them. A small squirrel, Ajidimo, hopped slowly to the front of the throng and stood in the middle of the great circle of her peers. "There should be a race," Ajidimo said. "A race would show who exemplifies the qualities of leadership. A race requires perseverance, fortitude, strength and a powerful will."

The circle of animals launched into a babble of discussion. Everyone was excited by this new possibility and, of course, many of the animals came forward to enter the race.

"It will be me," said Horse. "With my fleetness and strength I will overcome any challenge and I will emerge the leader."

"You think too highly of yourself, my brother," said Buffalo. "It will be me who emerges victorious, for no one has more stamina than me."

"What's needed is a discerning manner," said Cougar. "Your power is no match for my ability to cover territory with stealth. I will emerge as the leader because of my gift of patience."

"None can match my stealth," said Wolverine. "No one knows how to move secretly as well as me."

When no one else came forward to challenge these four, Eagle, who declined to enter the race because of her role as Messenger, carrying all prayers to Creator, called for quiet. She flapped down from the topmost branches of the tree she'd been sitting in and conferred with Makwa the bear and Ma'iingan the wolf. They talked a long while. Finally, Eagle hopped into the centre of the circle and addressed the throng.

"There is a lake set between a circle of steep hills," Eagle said. "I have flown over it many times and have seen that it forms a perfect circle. The terrain is challenging, rocky and steep, with thick woods around it. The race will be four times around that lake. This will demand the utmost of the contestants and the winner will indeed be the hardiest and most qualified to lead us."

The Animal People concurred that this was a remarkable plan. There was much excited talk about who of the four would emerge victorious. Then Eagle spoke again.

"Are there any other challengers? Is there anyone else who would like to contest for the right to lead us?"

"I would," said Waabooz the rabbit. She hopped out of the throng and sat looking at Eagle.

"You are small, my sister. Are you certain?" Eagle asked.

"Yes," Waabooz said. "It would be an honour to contest with such magnificent beings."

The animals worried that Waabooz was asking too much of herself but she was determined and the five contestants headed off for the lake with Eagle flying overhead as their guide. When they reached the lake Eagle lined them up on the rocky shore. "Be careful," Eagle said. "I have never seen any of us try to navigate this lake before. The terrain is so difficult."

The bigger animals stamped their hoofs and clawed at the shore impatiently. Waabooz merely wriggled her nose and watched them. At a signal from Eagle they took off and the race was on.

Horse neighed and reared up on his hind legs and then galloped off into the trees. Buffalo was right at his tail and the others could hear them crashing through the brush. Wolverine scurried forward in a low prowl with his nose close to the ground and vanished like a shadow into the forest. Cougar loped easily after him and disappeared as well into the thick cover of the bush. Waabooz sat on her haunches and watched them leave and, when she was ready, hopped off slowly into the trees too. Eagle flapped up to a pine growing on a ridge of rock to count the laps as they passed.

Horse and Buffalo were immensely strong and they made it back to the rocky shore in a virtual tie. They were scratched and cut from thrashing their way through the dense cover. They stopped to drink, and then Cougar and Wolverine bounded out of the trees as well. They all drank and caught their breaths and stared at each other to determine who might be wearied, weakened or want to drop out. None of them did and they raced off on the second lap. Eagle stared back in the direction they'd come from and worried about the tiny rabbit, who still could not be seen. The larger animals had returned from their second lap and then raced off again before Waabooz hopped slowly from the trees.

"Oh, the land is so lovely," Waabooz said. "There is so much to see and the feeling of being on it is beautiful."

"You are far behind," Eagle said. "There is no way for you to ever catch up."

"Don't worry about me. I'm here to enjoy the challenge,"

Waabooz said. Then she took a small drink and continued on her way.

Eagle waited a long time for that third lap to conclude. It was Buffalo who emerged first but even his proud steps were plodding. The great animal slumped to the shore and drank thirstily, his breath between slurps coming hard and heaving. When he finished, Horse walked out of the trees. He too was worn out. They stood side by side at the water's edge while Wolverine and Cougar walked out of the dense cover together. Wolverine and Cougar slung sidelong glances at each other but both were far too weary to comment or to challenge the other. Instead, they stood beside the other two animals and drank slowly. When they were finished, none of the great creatures seemed too eager to continue the race. They stared at the trees blankly until finally Horse stepped out first. The others watched him go and only when he'd vanished into the bush did they move to follow. Eagle could only peer back wondering how Waabooz was doing on her second lap.

The others had been gone almost an hour before she hopped out of the trees. She was bright-eyed and energetic and none of her fur had marks of struggle like the others. Again, she took a few small sips of water and sat on the shore admiring the look of the sun off the lake's surface.

"There is no way for you to win, my sister," Eagle said. "The others are on their final lap already. Perhaps it's best if you concede and stay here and wait to greet the winner along with me."

Waabooz nodded solemnly and continued to stare out at the lake. "It is not honouring the challenge if I should stop," she said. "It is a noble pursuit and it asks everything I have. So I will continue if that's all right with you."

"Certainly," Eagle said. "I only meant to spare you unnecessary struggle."

"It can never be a struggle to engage in a noble cause," Waabooz said.

She hopped off after the other creatures. Eagle flapped her great wings and settled more firmly on the branch. She admired Waabooz, who was brave and respectful and had a very humble way of looking at the world. She would have made a remarkable leader.

As Eagle sat in the tree, Waabooz ran nimbly along under the snags and tangles that hampered the bigger creatures. When she came to huge boulders she sat and sniffed at the wind and found the air currents that told her of the easiest path to follow. Where the way seemed impassable for someone of her size she merely sat up on her haunches and eyed the territory until she found a pathway. She'd established a route on her first two passes that allowed her to pick up speed. She blazed through open stretches and hopped boldly along the edges of chasms that seemed impossible for a creature so small. But she also took time to stop and admire the geography she passed through. She sat and gazed around at the magnificent sweep of country and hauled the crystalline air deep into her lungs. She admired the interplay of shadow and light that was thrown everywhere it is in the

# JOURNEY

*that one*

# BECOMES

# WISE

around her. Then she wriggled her nose and continued on her journey.

She hadn't gone far on her third lap when she encountered Wolverine. He was snagged in a crevice of rock where he'd been trying to take a shortcut over a ridge. He was furious and Waabooz could hear him snarling and raging and tearing away at the rock with his long claws. But he was also very tired and had to stop occasionally to catch his breath. It was during one such lull when Waabooz spoke to him.

"Let go," she said. "All you have to do is let go and stop struggling. When you do, you will slide back down and you can begin again."

"What do you know, little one?" Wolverine snarled. "I am strong enough to claw my way out of here."

With that, Wolverine attacked the face of the crevice again. There was an awesome sound of claws on granite and his hard spit and snarl. But it was to no avail. He was trapped.

"Let go," Waabooz said again. "It may require all your strength to do that, but your struggle itself is what traps you."

Wolverine huffed. His breath was ragged. He peered down at Waabooz, who seemed so small at the foot of the drop. It was a long way down. He gazed up at the thin strip of blue sky at the head of the crevice and he could feel a burning desire to breach it and continue the race. But he was exhausted. He took another look at Waabooz and she seemed so calm and assured that he relaxed and quit fighting. Sure enough Wolverine slid slowly back down the crevice and landed in the gravel beside her. He flopped down on his belly and stretched his paws out. "Thank you" was all he had breath for.

Waabooz sat and waited while Wolverine regained his strength. Eventually, he sat up. "It is lost," he said. "I am too tired to continue. I will not be the leader. I do not have what is required."

"The way I have found is easier," Waabooz said. "It takes longer but I make it all the way around without a struggle. I would be very happy if you accompanied me."

With that Wolverine and Rabbit began to make their way. They hadn't travelled very far when they heard a great stamping and snorting in the trees. They followed the sound and came upon Horse tangled in a thicket of blackberry bushes. The thorns were cutting into his flesh and the pain drove him to kick and buck relentlessly. He was covered in sweat. Again, when Horse ceased his immense struggle and had calmed some, Waabooz spoke.

"The branches are individual," she said to Horse. "If you pass through them one at a time there is less resistance. Taken together they are too strong a barrier."

"What do you know?" Horse asked. "You are not even in contention in this contest."

"That is true, but I know that barriers such as this are built of many parts," Waabooz said. "When I hopped through them I learned to be patient and push against one piece at a time. We will show you."

Rabbit led Wolverine to the edge of the thicket. She paused

and directed Wolverine to place his paw against one slim branch. A line of blackberry shoots fell forward. Then she hopped farther and showed Wolverine where to place another paw. More of a pathway opened up. Eventually they worked their way right up to Horse, who neighed in relief and followed them back out through the opening. When they stood in the clearing again, Waabooz and Wolverine could see how many cuts Horse had inflicted on himself in the thicket.

"Buffalo and Cougar passed by me and did not stop to help," Horse said. "That angered me. I fought against the bushes and they would not relent."

"Things bend any number of ways," Waabooz said. "You learn this when you spend time close to the Earth, as I do."

"Thank you," Horse said.

"We are travelling together now," Waabooz said. "The way I found is easier to navigate but takes more time. You're welcome to join us, of course."

"I'd like that," Horse said. "I'm very tired."

The three of them ventured off with Waabooz hopping casually along in the lead. Waabooz led Wolverine and Horse on a path that wound its way gently around and through many barriers. They were grateful for the respite. But they hadn't gone far when they heard Buffalo snorting angrily. They followed the sound and came upon him belly deep in a bog. Buffalo kicked and thrashed but his efforts only sank him deeper into the slick, oily muck. When he saw them on the edge of the bog he stopped and looked at them.

"How did you come to be in there?" Horse asked.

"I thought it was a shortcut," Buffalo said. "Cougar was bounding ahead of me and I thought that I could save time by cutting through a clearing. I was belly deep before I knew it."

"Can you stand?" Waabooz asked.

"Yes," Buffalo said. "Why?"

"If you stand there calmly you won't sink any farther and we can work together to get you out of there."

"Are you certain?" Buffalo asked. "I feel the bog pull at me even now."

"I am not certain," Waabooz said. "But Trust does not require certainty."

With that she hopped to a clutch of cedar trees and worked her way among them. Horse and Wolverine followed her and watched while she searched about. She came to a tree that had a root showing above the soil. Waabooz chewed at the root and when she'd eaten through it she asked Wolverine to come and dig at the ground with his great claws. He pawed at the soil and exposed a good length of root. Then Rabbit directed Horse to take the exposed root in his teeth and back up slowly to pull it from the ground. When he did this they could see that there was enough root to reach out to Buffalo where he stood mired in the muck.

"Take this in your teeth and swim out to Buffalo," Waabooz said to Wolverine. "Have him take it in his teeth and climb up on his back. Horse will pull you both out."

"But I might sink before I reach him," Wolverine said.

THE LIFE FORCE
*exists*

IN ALL
*things*

"Perhaps," said Waabooz. "But everything asks Sacrifice of us. You must sacrifice your doubt now to help your brother."

"Are you sure?" Wolverine asked.

"No," Waabooz said. "But I am not the one who has to be."

Wolverine took the root in his teeth and waded into the mud. He felt the mud clutch at him but he worked his way slowly toward Buffalo, and when the great beast took the root in his mouth, Wolverine climbed onto his back. Slowly, Horse backed away from the edge of the bog. Horse and Waabooz could see Buffalo and Wolverine moving closer and closer to safety. Finally Buffalo's hoofs caught and he struggled but soon walked out of the bog and stood there glistening with muck. Wolverine hopped from his back and did a celebratory dance around his larger brother.

"How did you know to find the root?" Buffalo asked.

"You discover much when you learn to look at things," Waabooz said.

Buffalo nodded. "I suppose Cougar has finished the last lap. He will be our leader now. I'm exhausted. I don't know if I can make it back."

"We have been making our way around together on the route that Waabooz found," Wolverine said. "It is longer but less arduous than the ones we followed. You're welcome to join us as well."

Buffalo agreed and the four friends resumed their loop around the lake. They came upon Cougar flopped on a large flat boulder, clearly exhausted. He lay on his side with his tongue lolled out, breathing in slow, shallow pants. His fur was matted and torn from negotiating his way through the territory, and his eyes were half closed.

"I'm spent," Cougar said when they approached him. "I went too fast for too long and the effort has robbed me of all my strength. I don't know if I have the energy to stand, let alone make it to the finish line. I've failed."

"There is no failure when judgment does not exist," Waabooz said softly.

"What do you mean?" Cougar asked.

"I mean that we do not judge you. We competed with you and we have no judgment. Neither does Creator. So it is not possible for you to have failed."

"But I did not complete the journey."

"—yet," Waabooz said. "We will carry you."

Buffalo stepped up to the rock and Cougar eased onto his broad back and the five of them continued their walk around the lake. Waabooz led them along and they marvelled at the leisure they found in the route she had discovered. When Buffalo's energy flagged, he moved beside another high boulder and Horse allowed Cougar to climb onto his back. Eventually, even Wolverine was near collapse, and Buffalo carried him and he rested his head on his brother's great hump. Waabooz hopped nimbly along ahead of them. Together, the five contestants walked slowly and evenly back to the shore where Eagle waited. When she saw them she flapped her great wings in celebration. They crossed the finish line together.

"It is a great day," Eagle said when told of Waabooz's direction.

"But we do not have a leader," Wolverine said.

"I think we do," Eagle said, and they all looked at Waabooz.

"Oh, I do not want to be the leader," Waabooz said.

"But you entered the contest," Buffalo said.

"I entered to learn what I did not know," said Waabooz. "I did not enter to contend."

"What was it you sought to learn?" Horse asked.

"I understood the meaning of leadership," Waabooz said. "But I did not understand the territory."

"And now?" Eagle asked.

Waabooz wriggled her nose. "I understand that when all our energies are directed toward the same goal there is no need for one to lead. We all help each other complete the journey."

"You are wise," said Eagle.

"I am Waabooz," she said. "That is all I know for certain."

"Then you are truly wise," Eagle said, and the others murmured their agreement.

Waabooz hopped off toward the line of forest at the end of the beach.

"Where are you going?" the others all yelled together.

"To complete the journey," Waabooz said. "I have one more lap to go."

"But there is no need," Buffalo said.

"But there is much I have not seen or learned," Waabooz said. "It is in the journey that one comes to understand the territory. It is in the journey that one becomes wise, and I have one more lap to go."

They watched her disappear, and after they'd drunk their fill of water and rested they stood at the break in the trees and waited while Waabooz completed her trek around the lake. When she returned, they welcomed her and Eagle scooped her up in her strong talons and placed her on Buffalo's back. They walked together back to the Animal People bearing a great story and a great Teaching.


EVERYTHING BEGINS WITH humility. The great circle of energy that comprises our being is driven by it. Without the guiding energy of humility, all other spiritual principles are diminished. It's possible to learn them, to practise them, but their vital foundation, their best intent, does not function as highly without humility at the helm. In the Long Ago Time, as the legends say, the Animal People existed with humility at their core. They spoke to each other as equals. They helped each other. When new beings appeared among them they sought to help, to guide, to teach. There was no hierarchy. They did not need hierarchy because the spiritual byproduct of humility is sharing.

My people say that for every spiritual principle there is a byproduct. That newly created energy is most always an action, a motion that is *energized* by the principle. In the case of humility, it is sharing. Sharing is not about goods or food or money. Rather, its intention is the stuff of the spirit—understanding, empathy, compassion, love, kindness, honour—and when something is shared from the spiritual

THERE IS NO
*ending*

WE ARE
*eternal*

wellspring, it is offered unconditionally. That is the true nature of giving: humbly offering in recognition of all that makes us kin. One energy, one drum.

Humility's energy is the binding agent that holds all things together—the glue, if you will. When we look at Mother Earth, we are looking at a truly humble being. She offers life to everything. She grants us her skin so we can grow crops. Her hair, the trees and vegetation, allow us to breathe. Her tears are the rains and the waters that gather as lakes and rivers, and they cleanse everything they touch and rejuvenate the life force that exists in all things. Her heartbeat resonates in all things and when we learn to listen, we are always able to feel it, and we are returned to the innocence we were born with, to that place of all beginnings where everything becomes possible. That is the nature of a truly humble being, and she is why Indigenous people have always said that the Earth is our university—we learn all things from her example.

When the Teachers of the Ojibway people were looking for an ongoing example of humility in action they did not need to look any further than at the world around them. Mother Earth has always been an enduring example of how humankind needed to live to survive: humility in action. The original instruction, "walk gently upon the Earth and do each other no harm," was given to the human family to direct their vision toward the workings of the planet, which were the highest expression of that dictum.

And so we are human—of the Earth.

Ojibway teachings say that all of us, the human family as expressed in the word *Anishinabeg*, come from the Earth. We emerge onto the breast of her as spiritual energy embarking on a journey to find the highest possible expression of ourselves. Our truth. With humility as our guide, the journey is less a trek than a perambulation toward the recognition of ourselves as Sacred. We are part of everything. We are part of Creation. Creation is a sacred flow of energy and we are part of that. To know yourself as a sacred part of Creation is to carry Humility.

My people say that when Creator blew life into the universe, it was with one breath. Creator took a shell and exhaled through it one time. Everything in Creation came to exist on that one Sacred Breath. Everything. All things became alive, flowing with energy, and that energy drew its force from the Sacred Breath. When we are born the very first thing we do is breathe. Then we feel. Then we cry for community. Then we reach out for it with both arms. It is the energy of that Sacred Breath that makes this so. All of us exist on one breath and my people say that because of that there is no ending; we are eternal. In the breath we draw today are the exhalations of every ancestor that ever lived. In the breath we draw today are the same drafts of air taken when Galileo came to understand that the Earth moved around the sun, when Jesus walked and when the first drum was brought to the Ojibway. Everything is joined. Everything is connected. Everything is part of that first sacred act and it means that we are all sacred—living and

WE ARE ALL
*one soul*

breathing on the one eternal Sacred Breath that infuses all things. This is what my people say, and in quiet times when I ponder that, I feel the truth of it and I am humbled.

But it is not always that simple. Life has demands. Life comes with the weight of expectation and responsibility. We feel pushed to achieve, to do, to become, to control, and those actions and compulsions are physical ones; they are not of the spirit. Instead, they are of the mind, because we think we should be taking action to be and to do and to have. We need to be industrious, we say, we need to do the things that are necessary so that we can have the things that will make us happy. The whole of human history has been built on this thinking and it has caused great harm to the planet. That thought pattern asks us to move beyond humility into the realm of thought and thus, that of ego and, ultimately, of fear—the fear of not having enough, of judgment, of failure.

But recognition of the Sacred Breath that joins us asks something more of us. It asks us to flip that thought pattern on its head. It asks us to change the essential way we view the progress of our lives. It asks us to simply be happy first. It asks us to actively choose that, because choice, in the Ojibway world, is the spiritual action that sets all energy in motion. When we choose to be happy first, we can do anything, and we will have everything we need because we are already happy. That is the great secret that lies at the heart of humility.

Like the Earth. The planet does not ask for certain conditions to be in place in order to fulfill herself. She simply *is.* We get so busy trying to be a certain way that we tend to forget what we essentially *are* at any given moment. We are alive. We are part of Creation. We exist on one Sacred Breath. We are Sacred. We are all one energy. We are all one soul— and the degree to which we forget this is the precise degree of separation that divides us.

## THE FIRST CEREMONY:
# The Sacred Breath

BREATH IS AN unconscious action. It happens of its own accord. When we emerge into this reality, breathing is the first act we perform as independent living beings. Our lungs fill with the Sacred Breath and we cry for contact. In fact, our entire journey on the planet is marked by two remarkably interconnected things—the will to keep breathing and the yearning for physical and spiritual contact. When we feel lonely we allow our rational minds to tell us that we are missing a person or a place. In truth, what we pine for is contact itself—the feeling of being with some person or at some location. Loneliness is a feeling that indicates the absence of a feeling: the special, life-empowering energy of connection that is a hallmark of our human condition. When we feel lonely we are telling ourselves that we are *out of the loop* and we miss the feeling of being in that specific circle of energy—the loop—we pine for. It is a spiritual malady and as the elders say, it requires a spiritual solution.

In the Ojibway world, as long as we breathe we carry Creator within us. There is no separation between us and our Creator. There is no spiritual journey required to find a point of contact, no elaborate system of faith, no necessary rites or commandments. All we need to do is breathe to know that our Creator resides within us and always will. The teaching

AS LONG AS WE
*breathe*

WE CARRY
*Creator*
WITHIN US

is that because we are joined by the one Sacred Breath there can never be separation. We are joined eternally to Creator and therefore to Creation. To be lonely is to not have been given that teaching or to have forgotten it. Because when you accept that you are a sacred part of everything, no greater and no lesser than anything, you are accepting that you can never truly be separate, that the flow of the nurturing, empowering and healing energy of Creation is within you and around you at all times. You are accepting that those people and places you miss are borne within that same flow of energy, and all you need to do is consciously connect with that energy to be unified, to be in harmony, to be joined.

The elders and spiritual people of First Nations recognized that it was a feeling of disconnection that haunted most people. They saw that we as a species become so busy, so involved with the physical act of our living, that we forget it is impossible for us to invoke disconnection. We are so engaged in being that we forget how to simply *be*. So they sought a means to allow us to remember that we are constantly a part of everything. They sought a way to help us reconnect whenever we chose. They sought a path that would lead us always to recognition of the great fact of our physical reality—that everything is energy, including us, and we can never truly be separate.

So the teachers created *ceremony*.

Much is made of that word. In the minds of people of all cultures and backgrounds it has come to mean a solemn, profound act that represents the faith we carry for a system of belief. Ceremony has come to mean the black-and-white expression of our obedience to the dictates of what we have come to recognize as truth. Most of the time it is regarded as *sacrosanct*, a ten-pound English word that means "exempt from question." To be followed to the letter. Or else. Ceremony, ritual, has become a measure of our faith, our belief, our worthiness, and as such, it has become a measuring stick for how Native we are, how Christian, how Muslim or Catholic. Ceremony has become fraught with judgment: the idea that whoever our God might be, He requires absolute adherence to the way, to the means, of approach. But those reactions are based on fear, and they're inaccurate.

The elders say that Creator is perfect loving energy. Within the realm of perfect love there is no judgment. If there is no judgment then there can be no failure. In turn, if failure does not exist, there is no unworthiness. We are all one energy. We are worthy and we always were. We never have to qualify. And ceremony was born to allow us to remember that.

A ceremony is simply a way to bring our energy into the great flow of creative energy that is the universe. As Indigenous people, every time we smudge with the Sacred Medicines, when we pray, meditate, enter a sweat lodge, do a Sun Dance or attend a Pipe Ceremony, we allow ourselves the opportunity to bring our energy into the loop. Truthfully, our energy always is in the loop, but ceremony was created to allow our minds, those busy beehives of disconnect, to remember that spiritual fact. The process, the protocol, was created for our minds—to give them

WITHIN THE REALM OF
*perfect love*
THERE IS
*no judgement*

something to grasp, to think about, to measure, to weigh and to lend importance to—because the teachers knew that as humans that's the way we're born. Headfirst. But ceremony itself was created for our spirits, for our hearts. Ceremony evolved so that we could *feel* it. The heart following the head into Creation.

Ceremony is a way to allow our emotional energy to encounter the wonder, the awe and the reverence that comes from an encounter with the divine, the sacred. It is a road to the true nature of our selves. It is a human process to a spiritual awareness—an awareness that we are sacred, that we are never separate from Creation or Creator. Ceremony is an emotional connection to that truth.

So this first ceremony is called the Sacred Breath Ceremony. It is one that can be done at any time but it is most useful first thing in the morning before we do anything else. When we awake, we emerge from darkness into light—the metaphor for life. Before our minds kick in, we are in a state of innocence, however briefly.

Find a place where you can be alone. It might be in your bed, propped up by pillows. Perhaps you have a room devoted to meditation or maybe there's a favourite place to sit where you always feel good. Go to that place. Make yourself comfortable. Remember that there is no right way or wrong way to do this. Instead, find your own way to this ceremony; go to the bathroom, drink some water, check in on the kids, whatever you need to do to give yourself unencumbered time alone. When you have finished that and you are seated in your comfortable place, you are ready to begin.

Relax. Let go of all tension or expectations or plans. Close your eyes. Breathe. As you breathe, allow yourself to feel the process. Notice the way the air feels coursing through your nose or through your mouth. Feel the swell of your chest as it fills your lungs. Feel the way your muscles and your ribs react. Feel the quiet and the stillness all around you. Relax and try to pull your breath deeper into you, into your diaphragm, into your centre. Breathe this way quietly until you feel the rhythm of your breath, slow and measured. Then allow your exhalations to sound. Push your breath out through your open mouth and listen to the way it sounds. Breathe in this way until you are relaxed with it.

Now, allow one thought to be present: *I am one with Creation.*

In and out, slowly breathe and allow that one thought to be present. Over and over again. Allow yourself to sink into it completely. Allow yourself to feel the power of this simple ceremony. Other thoughts will try to enter your consciousness. When they do, exhale, inhale and start over. Breathe in this way until the thoughts crowding in become too hard to push away. When you start to struggle, stop, and open your eyes. Every day try to extend the time spent in this ceremony a little longer. Every day try to push deeper into the feeling of the ceremony. Eventually you will build up your ability to sustain your Sacred Breath and to delve deeper into it, quicker. Your ceremony time will be as long or as short as you need it to be.

If you have incense or smudge you can light it prior to the ceremony. You can light a candle. But do not use music or

FIND A *place* WHERE YOU CAN BE *alone*

chants. The purpose is to remind you that you carry the Sacred Breath of Creation, to hear it, to feel it, and it is best to perform this ceremony in silence. You can always choose differently, because that is your right, but it is most beneficial to do it in a silent way. If you want to pray, do it after the ritual. Do it when you have felt the impact of the ceremony, because that is the purpose here—to feel.

When you are finished, move slowly and gently into your day.


THIS CEREMONY ALLOWS you to find your centre first thing in the day. It allows you to connect with your feelings and to feel the sense of awe and wonder that comes with a spiritual connection. It allows you to recognize the Sacred Breath of Creation within you and to carry the truth of that out into the world with you. It will change the way you feel and behave in the scurry of your daily life. Later, as you become more proficient, you can choose to do this ceremony as the day progresses: at your desk, on the bus, during your lunch hour or any other time you choose. But if there is one choice that empowers more than any other, it is finding time to walk to an open stretch of ground. As you walk there, consider why you're going and what you are about to do. When you get to your favoured spot try not to think about other people watching. Just allow yourself to breathe. By taking ourselves to the land, to a place where we can feel the Earth, we put ourselves in a place with the greatest flow of energy and the ceremony becomes even stronger. So once a week at least, build a walk into your schedule and do the ceremony outdoors. It is a spiritual gift you will give yourself.

The Sacred Breath Ceremony will let you feel humility. You will feel a part of everything. You will feel joined and connected and that feeling will change how you live your life and how you treat the planet.

But remember that the spiritual byproduct of humility is sharing. When you are comfortable with the ritual, when you feel an emotional attachment to it, when you feel that it is indispensable to you, bring it to other people. Tell your co-workers about it. Tell your friends and family. Tell everyone in your circle of influence about the benefits of this wonderful, simple ceremony. Then, when you find the one or the two or the handful that want to try it—*do it together.*

Do it together.

Gather in a quiet place and do the ceremony together. With a few people or as many people as possible, close your eyes, breathe and think the one present thought: *I am one with Creation.* In this way, the great circle of energy that is the universe becomes stronger by virtue of all the energy consciously joining in. In this way there is unity and harmony even in the smallest of circles. The degree to which we can bring our energies into the great flowing circle of energy everywhere is the precise degree to which we eliminate separation and create harmony. When we do this we become Creators and we become capable of healing the planet that is our home. This is spiritual. This is truth. This is Indian.

WHEN I WAS rediscovering the path to my Native identity after years of dislocation through foster homes, adoption, alcoholism and cultural denial, I often met people who gave me guidance in a traditional manner. It was my first introduction, really, to the principle that energy attracts like energy. I yearned for insight, knowledge and connection to myself, and the universe responded by sending the right people at the right times. They were teachers. They showed me, most times by virtue of their living examples, how to express who I was created to be. It wasn't an easy path. I was courted by doubt and indecision and fear that I would not measure up or that I would be rejected by my own people because I did not carry a sense of myself. But there were always teachers.

One of them was a wonderful woman named Lorraine Sinclair. She started an organization in Edmonton called the Mother Earth Healing Society back in the 1980s, and when I came along she was a recognized spiritual and environmental leader. At that time I was confused. I wanted to do something vital about the issues surrounding my people. I was a journalist specializing in Indigenous issues and the things I saw and experienced saddened and angered me. I wanted to evoke change.

But the big picture was enormous. Whenever I considered it I didn't know where to put my energy first. As much as I wanted to be a vehicle for change, I couldn't determine the proper course. So I went to talk to Lorraine, as I did sometimes when I had questions. We were walking by a river and I told her how discouraged I was. I told her that I wanted to be a force for change. I wanted a better world, not only for my people but for everyone. She listened and walked silently. When we got a small inlet cut out by the current she stopped and bent over to retrieve a pebble. Then she looked at me and smiled and I knew she understood that I was sincere.

"This is how you change the world," she said and tossed the pebble.

It plopped into the water and we watched as the ripples spread out from the splash and ringed to the shore at our feet.

"The smallest circles first," she said. "The smallest circles first."

It took some time for me to grasp the implication of what she said and put it into the proper perspective for myself, but when I did I realized what an incredible gift my friend had given me. She was telling me to do what was doable and to do it right now. The smallest circles first. Because sometimes the face of change is huge, galactic, and trying to discern a method to implement it confounds us and we don't know where to begin. Generally, this is because we have been able to convince ourselves as a species that we are the highest order of beings in the world and that we should be able to conquer anything. We went to the moon, for gosh sake. We created technology that allows us to communicate instantly around the entire planet. The evidence of our greatness is everywhere. So we gallop gallantly into the fray, convinced that we can arrange things to suit us.

But we're often defeated by size. The scope of what's needed is too enormous and we sit and ponder and reflect and we're flummoxed that we can't solve the big issues.

We think we need to change it all at once. We're convinced that solutions are instantaneous because that's what we've come to expect of ourselves. Lorraine was telling me that the opposite was true. If I were to concentrate my energy on the things that were achievable right now within my circle of influence, change would happen. If I determined to act differently toward the people and situations in my stream of life, change would happen. Then, if I chose to believe, if I gave my thought energy to the process, it would stimulate and attract like energy. Small circles of influence would develop everywhere and more change would happen. That humble energy, the kind that says, "I will do what I can do right now in my own small way," creates a ripple effect on the world. I believe that's true and it's what this book is all about.

Take that first ceremony out into the world. Carry it to your small circle of influence. Share it. Send that energy out and watch as other small circles ripple outward from that. My people say that change is the one constant universal law—everything is affected by change—and the energy that propels it is humility, and humility's spiritual byproduct is sharing. When sharing happens, loads are lessened and results increase. When sharing happens, the great nurturing wheel of energy is further empowered. It begins with a humble effort—the smallest circles first.

Another teacher came along when I was trying to incorporate all of this into my daily life. His name was Jack Kakakaway. He was Saulteaux, or Plains Ojibway as they are sometimes called. He'd fought in a war, survived a bigger war with the bottle and returned to the traditional teachings he was raised with. When I met him I was desperately trying to be a proper ceremonial person. I was a classic overachiever. Everything I did I performed as exactly, as excruciatingly close to the proverbial bone as possible, and I did not allow myself the least forgetfulness or fallibility. I was a rigid ceremonialist. I'd become convinced that only through the application of strict protocol would my petitions and prayers garner the response I wanted. So I had every traditional and tribal tool imaginable to help me with my spiritual search. Jack watched it all with bemusement.

Once when I was helping him prepare for a simple ceremony, I arrived with all my Ojibway accoutrements. As I set it all out on a blanket he watched me. Then he asked me a question.

"Suppose you wanted to say an earnest prayer. You wanted to canoe out to a small island in the middle of a great lake to offer this prayer because that's the way you believe your prayer would be answered. You put all of your prayer articles in that canoe. You have your pipe, rattle, drum, smudge bowl, eagle-feather fan, your medicine, eagle-bone whistle, every sacred article of faith imaginable. Then you set out for the island. But suddenly a big storm blows in and the wind capsizes

THIS IS HOW YOU
*change the world*

THE
*smallest
circles*
FIRST

your canoe and all of your sacred things sink to the bottom of that lake.

"Suppose you swim frantically and barely make it to that island. You're cold and shivering and you have nothing. All of the things that you have come to determine as necessary for an earnest prayer to be heard are at the bottom of that lake. Now you really need a prayer. You look up to the sky and you ask Creation for help. But without your sacred things, will your prayer be heard?"

That's what he asked me. I actually had to consider it for a long time. Then I said, "Yes."

"Why?" he asked.

Again I had to take some time to reflect. "Because it's the earnest prayer that matters, the desire to be heard, the desire for communion. It's not the tools," I said.

He merely smiled and rubbed my head like a son. I have never forgotten that.

The intent of Ceremony is to allow us to experience the feeling of faith, of trust, in the guidance and direction of Creator. In the everlasting flow of Creation, of energy, Ceremony is the ultimate act of humility. Within it you leave behind the intense human need to think, to consider, to evaluate, to judge, to determine and to process. In fact, when the settlers first saw Indigenous people in North America performing all their various rituals it was so far beyond their established religious protocols their first thought was that we must have been out of our minds. Strangely enough, that's the truth of it. For ceremony to be effective, for its intent to succeed, *we must be out of our minds.* We need to be in our hearts. We need to be in our spirits. That's what Jack was telling me that day. Ceremony is the experience of leaving behind everything but your ability to feel, and the power of the experience is in the emotional energy we find, create or engage in. It's not in what we think about it.

The tools we need for communion are our feelings, our spiritual energy. Ceremony engenders feeling. Feeling— energy—attracts like energy. When we experience like energy we experience Creation, the feeling of communion, and it takes an attitude of humility to receive it. Everything begins with humility. The medicine power of ceremony, then, is humility, living with the heart, being out of our minds.


THE PLANET IS the epitome of a humble being. Our Mother Earth exists for the sole purpose of creating a haven for other beings, other life forms. She exists as a teacher to show by her living example the way to live a good life. Within the framework of expressing herself to her highest degree, Mother Earth shows us examples of humility in action. She shows us the principles of being. She shows us harmony, unity, loyalty, fidelity, trust, interdependence, forgiveness, compassion and empathy. When my people looked around themselves, they saw what a powerful force for learning the planet was. The teachers and spiritual leaders knew that Mother Earth herself was the mirror that

[ 85 ]

they were looking for to show the Anishinabeg how to lead good lives. When they developed ceremony they used the Earth as the foundation. There were no temples, no cathedrals, no grand edifices erected to show the world how much faith they carried or what good and faithful worshippers they were. The planet was the shrine. They took themselves out onto the land and sat on the breast of her. They allowed their feet to walk upon her and they allowed themselves the opportunity to feel her heartbeat through the articulation of ceremony. In this way, in this vital and physical communion with the planet, they entered her university and learned how humble a being our Mother Earth is.

Humble beings exist as a matter of fact. They do not draw attention to themselves. They exist quietly. They live simply and they simply live. As the Ojibway watched the Earth, as they learned her rhythms and her motions, they and other Indigenous people around the world learned that humility is the most powerful force in Creation. Out of humility spring the Teachings and out of the Teachings spring Principles. For if humility is the fertile soil from which all things sprout and grow, then Principles, those ongoing acts of humility— the relentless march to our highest possible expression of ourselves—are the vegetation of our being. One cannot exist without the other. For just as great trees use the Earth to anchor their roots, to sustain themselves, so too do the trees breathe in during the process we call photosynthesis and exhale in the process known as transpiration to create water vapour, which becomes rain that falls down to nurture the soil. It is a circle. It is never-ending. It is continuous. It is a humble relationship.

So humility engenders principles. Principles drive the relationship. The relationship sustains life. When the Wise Ones watched the Earth they saw that and sought to bring it to the people. It happened everywhere. All over the world, when people sat with the Earth they learned the same lessons. It wasn't just sagacity pertaining to the Ojibway or Indigenous North Americans exclusively. The great forgotten truth of our reality as a human species is that we all came from somewhere. We all began our cultural journeys somewhere on the planet and because of that we are all Indigenous to her. Everyone.

But we learned to use our minds. We learned to think, to rationalize, to know fear and to be protective. When we learned that, we learned separation. And as we practised separation we learned dislocation and disharmony. As civilizations developed on their various paths we learned to feel superior, we learned to control, we learned to use physical power, we learned to exercise our fear masked as progress—the wish for more power and control. Great empires were born and as they flourished the idea that we are all Indigenous, that we are all tribal people, vanished in the march toward progress. We learned to exist for the grand illusion—that we can control things on the planet. Out of that illusion sprang another. Its name was technology. We learned the magic of devices as instruments of control and we devoted tremendous thought energy to inventing more and more. But each invention moved the human family further

EVEN *difficulties* ARE GIFTS

away from the truth of itself—that we are all tribal people and we need each other.

When those with technology encountered those without the need for it, the latter were called savages. The myth of superiority allowed the technology owners to justify physical, emotional and spiritual invasions into the lives of the savage ones. The land had become a resource and as such came to represent greatness. So those with technology simply took the land that those without it lived on and used it to further fulfill their desire to control things. The story of the human family is the story of separation from the teachings of the planet, separation from each other and separation from the truth that we are all tribal peoples. That is what we were created to be. Returning to the implications of that teaching is the path to resolution of all difficulties. And that path is blazed by humility and, in turn, by principles: humility in action.

As the Wise Ones learned to see, the planet showed them the effect of principles in action. One of the first that they were educated in was Sacrifice. They looked at the other beings they shared the planet with and the Ojibway saw that Sacrifice was an essential spiritual energy. Mother Earth is rife with it. Plants become forage for grazing animals. Animal beings give their lives for the continuation of others. Sacrifice is universal and the Teachers recognized it as the essential principle in the perpetuation of the planet and life itself. They also learned that Sacrifice was the ultimate act of humility: the giving up of one form of energy to sustain another. So they built it into ceremonies in order that the people might learn from it and be empowered in their journey.

So every ceremony, every act of bringing our energy into the great eternal circle of creative energy, involved an act of sacrifice, an act of humility. Unlike the sacrificial acts of offering lives for the appeasement of God or gods, the gestures were meant to be practical ones, the surrendering of some human energy. For instance, the Teachers asked participants to bring tobacco as a sign of their commitment to the ceremony. It is a practice that continues to this day as people ask for prayers, blessings or specific ceremonial acts for their benefit. According to the Ojibway story of the flood, Sky Woman took shelter on the back of a turtle with a handful of animals including Loon, Beaver and Muskrat. Each of the animals took turns trying to swim to the bottom of the water to retrieve soil. Muskrat was the last to try. Muskrats never swim very deep. Most times they can be seen on or near the surface of the water, but he dove to the very bottom of the great waters anyway. He was gone a long time. Finally he was spotted floating on the surface. He had drowned. But in his paw he clutched some of the precious soil. Because she was a woman and therefore capable of giving life, Sky Woman recognized his sacrifice and breathed life back into Muskrat. Then she took the soil and rubbed it onto the turtle's back and breathed life into it too. She walked upon the turtle's back in wider and wider and wider circles and it grew and spread outward. All things sprang to life upon the turtle's back and the first plant that emerged was tobacco. Since that time tobacco has been used as an offering because it is special, the first plant, the first gift of regeneration to the people from Creator and Sky Woman. It represents the sacrifice Muskrat made so that life could continue.

The Teachers asked for tobacco as an offering because it meant that the people would have to sacrifice their time and energy to plant, grow and harvest it. They might have to sacrifice their possessions to trade for it. These days, people might have to sacrifice their hard-earned money to purchase it. Ultimately, tobacco is used as a ceremonial offering to teach of the necessity of sacrifice in the spiritual process. There is an act of sacrifice involved in participating in any ceremony or ritual. We must also sacrifice pride in order to make the approach in an honourable manner. Pride is the opposite of humility and releasing it allows the power of humility to govern.

In the rich soil of humility all things grow. The water that enriches the soil is principle and the spiritual byproduct of living a principled life is gratitude. Thankfulness comes with the recognition that Creator and, in turn, Mother Earth are responsible for everything that makes our lives purposeful and abundant. They are responsible for all gifts, however small, unmeasured or unnoticed. In the Ojibway way of seeing, a gift is an empowerment, something that allows us to travel further on our way to the highest possible expression of ourselves. In this way, even difficulties are gifts, even hardship, even sorrow or the perception of loss are gifts because they all have the energy within them to teach us something vital about ourselves and the nature of our lives in this reality. We forget that. It's human nature to forget that. But ceremony allows us to remember and ceremony allows us to embrace and use these gifts. This is the way the Teachers saw things when they created ceremony.

So the second ceremony is about gratitude.

## THE SECOND CEREMONY:
# The Tobacco Offering

THIS CEREMONY IS called the Tobacco Offering. Because tobacco was the first gift following the flood, the first sign that life would continue, tobacco plays a very elemental part in Ojibway life. It is widely used as a sign of thankfulness. Even outside of specific ceremonies, Native people offer small bundles of tobacco wrapped in cotton cloth as an indication of their gratitude for a kindness. These bundles are called tobacco ties and they are integral to this ceremony.

Many years ago now, I was living in a healing lodge for Native men on a reserve outside of Calgary, Alberta. It was called the Sarcee Old Agency Lodge at that time. It sat on a curve of the road above a small creek and below a series of rolling hills. I remember how quiet it was there and how clear the air felt and tasted. I'd been living in cities all my life and the chance to live awhile in the open country appealed to me. The Lodge was a place for men with addictions to come and learn to heal themselves through the practice of traditional teachings. There were other programs offered too, like AA and other contemporary teaching paradigms, but what struck me most deeply were the traditional teachings. They resonated within me. They felt true. They made me feel that wholeness and life without alcohol were possible. Every sweat lodge

ceremony, pipe ceremony and powwow we travelled to evoked strong emotional responses in me and I wanted to learn as much about them as I could.

There was a man who worked at the Lodge. He was a tall, lanky man who grinned easily and talked slowly and gently. He and his family lived in a small house tucked away in the trees. When he spoke to me the first time I felt accepted and I began to approach him with questions. He'd been raised traditionally in the ways of his Sarcee, or Tsuut'ina, people and he was humble and quiet about it. In the language of the Lodge he was my sponsor, but I always preferred the word *friend*.

The more we talked, the more I came to trust him. See, there were things within me that I had kept hidden for a long time. There were a lot of painful things from my childhood that I was afraid to allow out into the light of day. They sat in me like stones and it made any kind of movement hard. But I didn't know how to let them go. He sensed all this and he took care to let me begin the conversation about those things at my own pace. I trusted him. I found him totally unthreatening and this made it easier to speak of difficult things. Or at least, as much as I was capable back then.

After a couple months of sharing, he gave me a mission. I was to trek into town. I didn't have a car then so I would have to walk a good four miles to the nearest bus stop. Then I was to find a fabric store and buy two yards of whichever colour of cotton cloth appealed to me, along with some string. After that my mission was to buy a tin of tobacco and then return to the lodge. While I was performing these errands I was to think about the things we had talked about. I was also to think about the things I was thankful for. When I returned I went to his office and he took me for a long walk out onto the land. We stopped beside a stretch of the creek that followed a wide gravelled curve. It was brilliant—the sky was a perfect blue and there was a slight hint of breeze. He sat on a large boulder and handed me a pair of scissors.

"Find a place to sit that feels good to you. When you think of something that you're grateful for," he said, "take the scissors and cut a small square from the cloth. Put a pinch of the tobacco inside, twist it and tie it with the string.

"Sit longer and think of something else. Only think of thankfulness. When something you're thankful for comes along, do the same thing again. Do it until you can't think of any more. Then come to me and we will take your string of tobacco offerings and leave them high in a tree by the water. We will offer them back to Creation."

It seemed an odd thing to me but I wanted so much to learn and to be freed of the burdens I carried that I did as he instructed. I sat among a small clutch of boulders with my feet on a smaller rock that sat in the water. There were trees around me and it felt like a small nest. I sat there for hours. When I emerged I had a long string of tobacco bundles. I offered thanks for my health, for the clarity of my mind, for the full use of my senses, for my sobriety, for my new friend, for the teachings I was receiving, and in the end, when I was really into the energy of the ceremony, I offered thanks for the difficulties I had encountered and for what they were able to teach me. When I handed him my string of prayers—because that's what they were—he hugged me and I climbed a tall tree and left those prayer ties high in the branches.

We talked on the way back to the Lodge and I told him of the things I had included in each of those small bundles.

"When we're sick or at dis-ease," he said, "we forget how powerful a medicine gratitude is. Gratitude is expressing your belief in the existence of gifts, even those you can't see. So when you become thankful, you create a powerful energy and that energy goes outward and becomes a part of the greater energy all around us and you learn to heal. That is the nature of this ceremony.

"When you returned your thankfulness to the land, you were recognizing where it came from. It came from the ability to be humble—to see yourself as a sacred part of everything.

"Do this whenever you feel overwhelmed by things. Do it when you feel lonely. Do it when you are doubtful, or when you're afraid. Centre yourself on thankfulness all the way through and the ceremony will lead you to wholeness. It always will."

He was a good man. When I left the Lodge I took that teaching with me. Eventually I showed others how to perform this ceremony and I've done it in groups of upward of twenty people and each and every time it has been a powerful reconnecting experience. It has always allowed me to see my sacred place within Creation and because of that, it is the essence of humility. So it is your second ceremony.

Devote one whole day to gathering the articles you will need. Tell yourself that nothing will interfere with your sacrifice of time and money. Walk as much as you can in gathering these things. As you walk, focus on the fact that you are on a mission of thankfulness. Breathe. Allow the essence of this adventure to fill you. While you make your way around the stores and markets to fill your list, smile at people, make eye contact, but stay within yourself as much as possible without being rude or discourteous. The articles you will find are two yards of pure cotton cloth, in red, yellow, deep blue or white, a bundle of white string, a small pair of scissors and a thick blanket for you to sit upon while you perform the ceremony. Once you have everything together, return home and place all of the articles together in a safe, quiet place. Focus on them. Remember what they are to be used for.

That night eat a good substantial meal and drink a generous amount of water before bedtime. You will not eat or drink again until after the ceremony is finished the next day. If you like you may prepare a special personal feast for yourself for when you return, or pack a picnic bag to take along.

The next morning do the Sacred Breath ritual. When you are ready, make your way to the place on the land where you have chosen to sit and do this work. It may be in a park, it may be on a hiking trail, but make sure to choose somewhere on the land that feels peaceful and serene. When you find a place where you can sit quietly, spread your blanket out and place your articles within easy reach. Do the Sacred Breath ritual again. When you feel embedded in that sense of connection to the land around you, open your eyes and begin.

Begin with those things that come easily to you. Offer tobacco ties of thanks for your health, family, home, work, school, friends and possessions. Then breathe deeper and try to feel what other things in your world and experience you are grateful for. You will find lots when you are properly centred. Maybe you're thankful for having ten fingers and ten toes, to be able to hear, to see. Maybe there's a skill or an art you carry. Perhaps you're thankful for teachers in your life. The more you focus on the energy of thankfulness, the more things will come to you, and as each does, put a small pinch of tobacco in a small square of cloth and tie it with the string. Keep the string unbroken so that you create a long line of gratitude ties. Think of the tobacco as a sign of regeneration, of continuation. Keep going until you can't think of anything more. When you start to struggle with it, stop.

Find a place in a tree, beside some rocks or in a cleft in the vegetation that appeals to you and leave your string of offerings there. Say a prayer of thanks for the opportunity to do this ceremony. As you return home consider what you have just done. Consider how it felt to devote all that time to just being thankful. Consider how the feeling of gratitude affects you. Consider how you feel. When you get home, spread your blanket on the floor, offer another prayer of thanks and celebrate your feast, if you've prepared one. Later, when you've rested, take a piece of paper and write about your experience, concentrating on feelings more than thoughts or observations. When you're finished, phone a friend and make arrangements to share the story of your ceremony with them as soon as possible. When you have finished that, you have completed the Tobacco Offering because all ceremonies are only completed when they are shared.

During this time you will have learned and felt connection. By solely focusing on the intent of the ceremony you are gifted with insight: how you bring yourself to it. You learn that the approach to ceremony is quiet, peaceful and humble. In that atmosphere your preparations allow you to focus on the intent of the ritual itself. Inside that spiritual energy you come to have a relationship with the principle of gratitude; you learn how it feels to recognize and to carry it. When you emerge from that space you carry a physical sign of your thankfulness. You see it and feel it, and if you wear it around your neck while you search for a place to offer it back to the Earth, you sense its impact on you. Your energy has been ushered into the flow of healing energy. You've added to the well-being of the planet. You've taken care of the smallest circle first.

This is a very spiritual ceremony. But spirituality finds its greatest possible expression of itself in community. Once you are familiar with the protocol of the ritual, introduce it to the friends you introduced the Sacred Breath ritual to, or those who you know would appreciate it or would be willing to learn. Pick a spot where a group of people could go to do it together. Gather them around you and tell them about your experience. Give them directions on gathering their articles. Arrange to share a potluck feast at the conclusion. Gather in the morning and travel together to the ceremony site. Before everyone separates have a brief moment of calm. If your friends know the Sacred Breath ritual, do that together. If not, merely meditate together with your eyes closed. As they prepare to go out alone, tell them that there is no right way or wrong way to do the ceremony. Tell them that it is the earnest desire to follow it through that matters most. Then let them go and find their spot.

If there is the opportunity to light a small fire, take that role upon yourself. Have the fire burning all the while people are meditating and offering thanks. While you tend the fire, make your own string of offerings. As people return, have a drink of water ready for them. Then stand together at the fire and say prayers of thanks for the Tobacco Offering ceremony, either aloud or to yourselves. After that everyone can put their prayer ties into the fire, and it then becomes a Sacred Fire. In Ojibway teaching, this means that the fire burns and carries thoughts and prayers to the Spirit World, to the ear of Creator, to the ancestors, and thus becomes joined to the great wheel of creative spiritual energy. One by one, offer your ties to the Sacred Fire. When everyone is finished, join hands around the fire and offer a prayer of gratitude for the teachings that come from that ceremony as well. Each person can offer a

ceremonies
ARE ONLY
completed
WHEN THEY ARE
shared

prayer aloud if they choose. Once that is over move around in a circle and hug each other and offer thanks for being a part of the process. Then share your feast and water in a spirit of celebration before returning to your individual homes.

When you perform this ceremony as a group the flow of energy is greater. The larger the number, the greater the flow. With an increase in nurturing, healing energy, the universe responds with like energy, and the energy flow around the planet grows stronger and it is healed to the precise degree that participants allow themselves to believe that it is. As in all spiritual matters, it is the act of Allowing on our parts that sends the energy outward. So when we allow ourselves to believe and then act on that belief we allow an incredible amount of energy to flow outward. Collectively, we have the ability to allow even more.

Spirituality sees the highest expression of itself in community. As much as the Tobacco Offering is a profound personal experience, it renders even more power when more spirits are joined in the circle of it. Further, when people join together to articulate their belief, faith and energy, there is harmony. There is joining. There is community. The energy that comes from a simple ceremony like this brings us together in ways that few things can. When we join together in the Tobacco Offering we create a bond that can never be forgotten or breached. Our energies are linked forever. We shared the same Sacred Breath and the same spiritual energy and that is a sacred joining.

Within each of us is a shaman. Within each of us is a

teacher. Within each of us is a storyteller. These are powerful roles that are vital to our collective survival. Ceremony shared by a group empowers those roles and makes us capable of carrying them to others. When we do that the circle grows stronger and the potential for healing is enormous. If you decide to bring this simple ceremony to others you are embarking on the path of the shaman, the teacher and the storyteller. You are fulfilling your greatest destiny and you are coming closer to the highest possible expression of who you were created to be. That is the nature of ceremony. That is the power of humility. That is the promise of a principled life.

# ZOONGIDE'EWIN:
## courage

**Ernestina was** a field mouse with a reputation for having a troublesome curiosity. Unlike other mice who were content to mosey around using their whiskers as their guides, Ernestina wanted more. She wanted to *see* the world. She wanted to go beyond what her nose could tell her and use her eyes to determine things. The other mice did not understand such a way of life. They had grown up as all mice do, with an understanding of who they were and who they were created to be. To consider acting unlike a field mouse was odd and uncomfortable to them. But they loved Ernestina and stood by her despite her rampant curiosity, which they were sure would lead her to trouble.

Mice are notoriously shy. When someone new or different comes along they're willing to hide behind a root or a stone and allow the newcomer to pass so they can inspect and evaluate them. Their tiny whiskers work overtime trying to judge the intent of the new creature. But Ernestina would instead dash out to investigate and would sometimes just barely miss the snap of the jaws of a fox or the hard clack of an owl's talons. She'd sit and quiver in breathless excitement over these encounters.

"You're not behaving wisely," the older mice would tell her. "Our way is caution. If you go beyond that we may not be able to help you."

"But I want to see what exists in the world," Ernestina said. "I want to have experiences."

"Experience is a good thing. Done in a safe mousy fashion it allows you to grow in mousy knowledge. But dashing out into the open might spell the end of you," they told her.

Ernestina's heart, though, was an open one. She loved the smell of the wind and the sound of the grasses when it blew from the west. She loved the sight of the creatures who passed the meadow where her band of mice lived. She had a particular fondness for the taste of the varied plants she found on her solitary rambles to the edges of their territory. To Ernestina, the world was a place of sensation and she wanted to experience it as fully as she could. So she used her eyes to lead her around.

Now, a field mouse's whiskers and keen sense of smell are what lead them to food. But Ernestina wanted these senses to lead her to new visions instead, things neither she nor any other mouse had ever seen before.

"There are Teachings we have not known," she said to her best friend, Philomena. "As wise as the old mice are, there is a whole world out there and it's filled with Teachings and songs and knowledge that we can't get within the borders of our meadow."

"You're talking dangerously," Philomena said. "No mouse has ever dared wander beyond our borders."

"And no mouse has ever become more," Ernestina said.

"What more is there?"

"That's what I intend to find out."

So Ernestina began to explore. Every day she inched a few feet beyond the borders of the mouse meadow. It was heady

stuff. She tingled with excitement, and the feeling of danger that clutched at her belly was offset by the surge of wonder she felt at the sight of new things. She told no one of her forays. Instead, she dreamed at night of wandering far and away, and of splendid vistas and strange new creatures she would meet and speak with. She dreamed of new Teachings that she would bring back to the field mice and she pressed farther every day.

Using her eyes instead of her nose led her to amazing sights. She found a new kind of stone. It was dappled with colour and glinted in the flush of the sun. She discovered new plants and trees and stretches of water. When she found each new thing she sat in a safe place and drank the vision into her so she might describe it in great detail when she shared it with the other field mice. The world was becoming larger and was filled with great mystery, and Ernestina wanted to see even more of it.

One day when she was farther afield than she had ever been she came across a pond. The water was covered with flat green lily pads and its edge was a throng of reeds. Ernestina crept out onto the pebbles and smelled it and looked at it. The odour was strange. It smelled old and new all at the same time and she found that magical. Suddenly she was aware of being watched. At first she wanted to flee but her curiosity got the better of her and she began to try to see who might be looking at her. She found herself looking at a pair of eyes stuck up from the surface of the water. The eyes blinked lazily. Then they moved. They approached a lily pad inches from where she stood and a strange wet-looking green creature clambered out and sat there staring at her.

"I'm Omagakii," the creature said. "Frog, you can call me."

"I'm Ernestina. I'm a field mouse."

"What are you doing here at the pond?" Frog asked.

"I'm learning to see the world."

"That's a very big thing. Do you know how large the world is?"

"No. But I intend to find out."

"How far have you been so far?"

"Oh, a very long way," Ernestina said. "I've come from the mouse meadow all the way to this pond."

"That is a long way," Frog said. "Especially for such a small creature as yourself. But the world is huge. To learn to see it you would have to travel very, very far and it might get lonely."

"I'm not afraid to be alone. And how big could it really be? Have you seen it?"

Frog croaked. He blinked his eyes and launched his tongue at a passing fly. He missed, settled on the lily pad again and stared at Ernestina. "Well, no," he said. "I'm not the adventurous type, I'm afraid. A frog life is good enough for me. I admire your bravery. But I have heard stories."

"Stories? From who?" Ernestina asked breathlessly.

"Oh, there are many travellers," Frog said. "They stop here to drink now and then and I ask them questions and they tell me stories of their travels. There are many marvellous places to see in the world."

"What's the most marvellous?"

Frog croaked and pondered Ernestina's question. "Well, I imagine that if I were brave enough to venture out I should want to see the Magic Mountain."

Ernestina gasped. "The Magic Mountain. Wow. It sounds wonderful. Where is it?"

"Far to the west," Frog said. "It is a great journey. I only know of larger four-legged ones who have made it there, or great birds."

"I will make it there," Ernestina said.

"I don't doubt that you will. You seem of a very determined sort."

After that Ernestina could not get the idea of the Magic Mountain out of her head. It invaded her daytime thoughts and her nighttime dreams back in the mouse meadow. It went with her everywhere she travelled. Finally, she determined that if she were to see and experience it, she would need every ounce of bravery she had, because it would be a long and lonesome trek. She wondered if she had that kind of courage. When she realized that the desire to see and experience was greater than her fear, she prepared to go.

Philomena walked with her to the edge of the mouse meadow. "How long will you be gone?" she asked.

"I don't know. It is very far away."

"Will you come back?"

"I don't know that either."

"Then why go?"

"I need to see and experience the world."

"Why?"

"I'm not sure," Ernestina said. "I only know that I feel like if I don't I will not be as much as I can be."

"But you're a mouse."

"Yes. But I can be more of a mouse this way."

"I do not understand."

"Perhaps you will when I return and share the story of my travels."

With that, Ernestina gave her friend a big hug and set off west toward the Magic Mountain. She travelled many days. Every inch of territory was filled with new and exhilarating sights, sounds, smells and tastes and Ernestina forgot that she was alone. The world filled her being. She crept and scurried and poked her way west and she could feel excitement in her every inch of the way. Soon she came to the edge of the Great Plains. She climbed up on a rock and looked across the great sea of it. Where it ended at the hard blue edges of the sky was just a long, slowly undulating line of earth. It was enormous and captivating and she sat there a long time.

Soon she heard the clomp of feet on the ground. She dropped down to the edge of the rock and huddled there and looked out to see who might be passing. It was Horse. She'd never seen Horse before but she had heard tales of the creatures from other mice. When Horse lowered her nose to nibble at some fresh shoots, Ernestina called out to her.

"*Aaniin*," she said. "Hello. I'm Ernestina. I'm a field mouse."

Horse was startled and skittered off a foot or so but when she saw who was calling to her she settled and stepped closer. "I am Horse," she said. "What are you doing here at the edge of the Great Plains?"

"I'm going to the Magic Mountain," Ernestina said.

"That is many days off. It's dangerous for you to try to get there. There are many creatures who would enjoy a morsel like you."

"I'm not afraid. I really want to see and experience the world."

"That is truly a noble calling," Horse said. "Let me help you."

"How?"

"I'm travelling a few days to the west to see my cousins. I'll kneel down so you can scramble up onto my back. Hold tight to my mane and I will carry you as far as I'm going."

So Ernestina clambered up onto Horse's back and they began moving across the Great Plains. While she marvelled at the view Horse told her stories about all she had seen and experienced and Ernestina shared stories of her life. They travelled easily this way. They travelled four days. Eventually they came to the edge of a long draw.

"I go south from here," Horse said. "But if you keep going west beyond this draw you will begin to see the Magic Mountain."

Ernestina thanked Horse for her kindness and they went their separate ways. At the far edge of the draw Ernestina raised

herself up on her hind legs as far as she could and tried to see the Magic Mountain. She strained and strained but she could not see anything. Undaunted, she began to travel west again.

The blue of the sky was thrilling. The breeze that riffled the prairie grasses was filled with scents of flowers, trees and creatures she'd never met before. She could hear the twitter and call of birds whose songs were magical and filled her with longing and celebration. The trek was less arduous because of all the things in the world that surrounded her. She travelled in a daze. Her senses were afire with new inspirations. Then, after five long days, she stopped beside a clump of sage to rest. She loved the sharp tangy smell of the sage and it comforted her. She slept. When she opened her eyes she was staring into a pair of liquid amber eyes. They were wise with a touch of humour and Ernestina did not feel afraid.

"*Aaniin*," she said. "I'm Ernestina. I'm a field mouse and I'm going to see the Magic Mountain."

There was a low chuckle and the eyes flickered. "Well, that's admirable of you. I am called Coyote. This is my territory you've wandered into."

"Well, I shall treat it respectfully," Ernestina said. "You'll hardly even know I was here."

Coyote chuckled again and hauled himself up onto his haunches and gazed down at the mouse. "Why would such a small being as you risk everything to travel somewhere that might not even exist? One snap of my jaws and you'd be breakfast, after all."

"Oh, I'd be a poor meal," Ernestina said. "This journey has worn me very thin. You'd do much better elsewhere. And I know the Magic Mountain exists because my friends Frog and Horse told me so."

"Frog and Horse? Well, you've been well informed. However, it's a long way from here. It gets even harder after this. The land starts to toss itself into ridges and gullies and canyons and a young mouse like you would be hard-pressed to make it."

"I'll make it," Ernestina said. "It's my desire."

Coyote laughed. "Desire, you say? What do you know of desire?"

"It's a heart song," Ernestina said. "It comes out of you all rich and pure and you don't know how it ever got inside of you. It stuns you and you can't help but follow where it leads you."

"Why, that's very wise," Coyote said. "When the full moon rises over the lip of the world I find a song in me like that and I just have to lean my head back and sing it. It's how I became Coyote."

"Yes," said Ernestina.

"Yes," said Coyote. "Listen, I'm travelling west. Why don't you climb on my back and I'll carry you as far as I'm going?"

"You would do that for me? What about breakfast?"

Coyote laughed again. "I am a great hunter. I will find a meal. What's important is that a brave and wise being like you gets to see her desire. Hop on."

So Ernestina settled into the thick fur of Coyote's ruff and he loped off toward the west. While they travelled Coyote filled Ernestina's ears with great tales of trickery and mischief and she found herself laughing until her sides hurt. Coyote was a great storyteller. He was also a wonderful guide and took the time to point things out to her among the canyons and gulches they trotted through and explain their function in the great scheme of things. The world became marvellous through Coyote's words. Ernestina loved every sight and every sound.

"If all of this is so wonderful, I can't wait to see the Magic Mountain," she said to Coyote.

"In all the world there is no more beautiful sight," Coyote said. "It is worth all the difficulty of your journey to see it."

They trotted on a long time. Finally, they crested a small hill of grass and Ernestina gasped. There was a strange creature standing in the great emptiness of the prairie. Coyote stopped on the rise and they looked down at it. The animal was enormous. It was dark brown with huge humped shoulders, great horns and large hoofs. But what caught Ernestina's attention most were its eyes. They were a deep, dark brown and they were crying. She could almost hear the thud of the huge tears that kicked up plumes of dust when they hit the flat of the plain.

"It's so sad," she said.

"It is Bison," Coyote said. "He is a great Teacher."

They trotted toward Bison, who raised his head and sniffed

at the air. "Who is it that approaches?"

"It is me, my brother," Coyote said. "It is Coyote, and I bring a new friend from far away."

"Who is this friend?" Bison asked.

"My name is Ernestina. I'm a field mouse." She climbed down from Coyote's back and stood in front of the magnificent creature.

"A field mouse? You're very far from home."

"Yes. I'm going to see the Magic Mountain."

"That is a noble quest for such a tiny being. Why do you make this journey?" Bison asked.

"It is my desire," Ernestina said.

"Ah," Bison said. "You make a journey of the spirit. Noble indeed."

"Why are you crying?" Ernestina asked.

"My heart is sad," Bison said. "I have lost the use of my eyes and I cannot find my way."

"Where is it you need to go?" Ernestina asked.

"I need to find the People," Bison said. "They are hungry and I need to go and nourish them. But without my eyes I cannot find the way. Without me they will perish and that makes me very sad."

"Then take my eyes," Ernestina said.

"Why would you offer that?" Bison asked.

"Your journey is so much more important than mine. Please. Take my eyes and find the People and feed them."

"You are a very brave being," Bison said. "But how will you

find your way to the Magic Mountain then? How will you see its wonders?"

"I'm a mouse. I'll use my whiskers as mice do," Ernestina said. "When I get there I will feel it."

"You are wise," Bison said. "I would be honoured to accept your gift."

With that, Ernestina's eyes flew from her head and into Bison's. She could hear him clomp his great hoofs in celebration and snort in glee. Coyote yipped in delight too. Ernestina was very happy. But her two friends noticed her standing there sightless and small, sniffing at the air and moving her whiskers, and they became very quiet.

"How will you make it now?" Bison asked.

"I will take her there," a voice said from the sky.

Bison and Coyote watched as Migizi the eagle soared in and landed beside them. Eagle ruffled her feathers and stepped close to Ernestina, who wriggled her nose and moved her whiskers to sense who this new arrival might be.

"I am Eagle. I saw what you did for our brother and for the People in turn. That was a very brave and marvellous thing. I will take you to the Magic Mountain," Migizi said.

"You know where I want to go?" Ernestina asked.

"Yes. I flew from the east. Frog and Horse told me of your journey and I decided to find you and help you. I did not expect to find you so far away or to see you perform such a selfless act of courage. It would be my honour to fly you to the Magic Mountain."

"Thank you," Ernestina said.

"It is you we should thank," Migizi said.

"Take some of my hair," Bison said. "Wrap it around yourself so that Migizi's talons do not pierce you."

"Thank you," Ernestina said. "That is so kind."

"And take a tuft of my fur," Coyote said. "When you meet my cousins in the mountains show it to them and they will help you."

"I will miss you," Ernestina said.

"I will miss you too," Coyote said.

When she was ready, Migizi scooped Ernestina up in her talons and flapped off to the west. Ernestina could feel the wind on her face and she could hear the sound of the great wings flapping. While they flew Migizi told her stories of creatures she had met, of the People and how the animals had all agreed to help them find their way around the world, of Teachings she had gathered in her journeys and how the Magic Mountain itself had come to be.

"It exists in a place called Faith," Migizi said. "That means that it stands in a different place for everyone. But it is very real and all who travel there become more."

"I want to become more," Ernestina said.

"Yes," Migizi said. "That is the nature of the journey."

She soared downward in a long, broad angle and Ernestina felt the marvellous rush of air against her face. Migizi landed and set her on the top of a large, flat rock. "The Magic Mountain is right in front of you now. There are trees and rocks that obscure the view. But if you stand on your hind feet and stretch up as hard as you can you will be able to feel it. Push your nose as high as you can and you will sense it. Allow your intuition to guide you. Push as hard as you can, Ernestina."

The little mouse stood up on her haunches. She gathered all her strength. She summoned every ounce of desire. She imagined the Magic Mountain shining in the sunshine, its crest white with snow against the deep blue sky, its rock face ancient and wise. She craved the vision. She stretched as hard as she could. She could feel the strain on her skin but she pressed herself upward even more and when Migizi said to jump, she leaped upward and strained to get her whiskers as high in the air as possible.

She kept rising. She felt herself moving upward into the air. She was weightless and when she moved her front paws to find balance they became wings and she opened her eyes and saw that she was soaring in the crystalline air as a great brown eagle. She was high above the mountains and as she soared on her powerful wings and gazed down she felt great joy, and she cried at the sheer beauty of the world beneath her.

"How can this be?" she asked.

"Your bravery has made you more," Migizi said from beside her. "Your desire arising from the place called Faith has changed you. When you faced the challenge with integrity you embraced courage and when you acted out of that courage you engendered Faith itself—and you have become more. Now you are Golden Eagle, Ernestina. Fly and tell your story to all who will listen. Share your Teaching and allow others to become more too."

With that, Migizi soared off to the south and Ernestina, now a golden eagle, flapped off to the east to bring her Teaching and her story back to the mouse meadow where her journey began.

WITH HUMILITY AS its guide, Courage becomes a powerful energy. When you can see yourself as a Sacred part of everything that is, of all Creation, you come to realize that there is no separation, that the flow of loving and nurturing energy is around you constantly. When there is no separation, there is no end, only continuation. As a species we've come to believe in finalities. We have come to believe that everything ends. The cultural mythology that most of us share across the planet is that when life is over we go somewhere else. We believe this because we are given to believe that when we come out into this reality, onto this planet, or as my people say, this Earth Walk, we come here separate from Creator. But my people say that we always were and are a part of Creator. Because we exist on the Sacred Breath of Creation, separation does not exist. It never did. So there is no death. There is only continuation because we are a part of eternal energy. When you come to accept that, you can exemplify Courage as a life principle. Courage means that you can face a foe with integrity and the foe in our human

experience is fear. Fear is the absence of faith. Courage is walking with faith. In the context of this Earth Walk, having faith means that we are never separate, that there is no ending, no finality. It means that this experience is expansive and evolving and we will always be. We will always carry on.

I remember when I was in my mid-twenties, I had just found my way back to my people after twenty years of foster homes and adoption. I had spent the years from ages sixteen to twenty-four as lost as anyone could possibly be. When I left my adoptive home I left with only a completed grade nine and no job skills. I lived on welfare and minimum-wage jobs whenever I could find them. Sometimes when those jobs did not materialize, I lived on the street and frequented the missions, hostels and soup kitchens of the towns and cities that I wandered through. My life was a jumble of confused perceptions and I believed that I was not meant for any kind of fulfillment or satisfaction. I believed that if there were a God in the universe he must have been preoccupied when I really needed help and guidance. I made bad choices based on fear and landed in jail more than a few times. My fear ate at my belly and I learned to drink alcohol to numb it. I had no faith in anything and I was not a brave person.

When I rejoined my people in 1978, I discovered a wellspring of teachers, ceremonies and healers to guide me back to a perception of myself as a Native person. I hadn't known these treasures existed. When I went into foster care I was little older than a toddler and in all those years I was not offered a way to connect to my own people. I grew up feeling very much like a fence post in a field of snow—everything around me was white and I never felt like I belonged. But when I experienced my own culture and traditions, that feeling of alienation vanished. Suddenly I had ways of expressing who I was and I consumed them with all the enthusiasm of a starving man. But in my frenzy to learn and to become as Native as I could be, I missed out on a lot of the proper articulation and intent of the Teachings I was given.

As I learned the history of the settlement of North America and the displacement of my people and the other First Nations across the continent, for a time I became bitter and angry. There was a growing militancy among young people and I eagerly embraced it. There were marches and protests. There were office occupations and sit-ins. At the height of that energy there were violent confrontations and standoffs and I believed then that the things we were doing were justified and right. I believed that the answer to the forced subjugation of my people's identity, tradition and culture was force itself.

There was a mantra in those days that was said to have come from the great Lakota Sioux war chief Crazy Horse. Everyone in what we called "the struggle" walked with this mantra. It said, "Today is a good day to die." What we believed it meant was that, as warriors, we were prepared to lay our lives down for the people. We believed it meant that we would fight to the ultimate end. So we wore our red headbands, camouflage, fringed buckskin vests and moccasins with pride, bearing that very brave statement before us. Everywhere I went and met young First Nations people, "Today is a good day to die" was what brought us together.

I found myself at a gathering called the Indian Ecumenical Conference in Morley, Alberta one summer. A large number of traditional teachers and medicine people shared their Teachings and ceremonies with us there. Morley was *the* place to be seen if you were any sort of radical at all. The Teachings and the ceremonies were what we were bound to protect and being there when they were discussed and practised was the ultimate show of worthiness. So I managed to get there.

There was a spirit and energy to the gathering that made me uncomfortable. I felt *wrong*. That's the best word I can use to describe my anxiety. As I sat in sessions and participated in rituals I felt invalid and the feeling of prayerfulness and humility was overwhelming. Because I was not a brave person, I reacted out of my adopted militancy. Whenever I felt challenged I simply said the magic words of inclusion that I knew by heart. Today is a good day to die.

One of the teachers overheard me one night. His name was Albert Lightning. He was Cree and a highly regarded ceremonialist and teacher. He approached me when there wasn't anyone else around and asked me to sit with him. When we were comfortable he looked at me for a long moment. "What are you so afraid of?" he asked.

He asked it directly and simply without an ounce of judgment in his voice. Instead, he sounded concerned and compassionate.

"I'm not afraid of anything" was what I said in reply.

He nodded and stared at the ground and reflected on my words and when he looked back up at me again there was an earnest and open expression on his face. "What you said over there, those words, do you know what they mean?"

I gave him the stock militant answer and he merely nodded again. "When Crazy Horse was with us," he said, "he was a great leader. He was very brave. He spent a great deal of time with spiritual people and learned the principles and values that make a leader great. He took the time to learn the foundation of the warrior way and that foundation was always spiritual.

"When he used the words 'Today is a good day to die,' he did not mean that he was so brave that he could go into battle and give his life without question. He meant that he had actually considered the questions. He meant that before he took up his war lance he had spent time in meditation and prayer. He had looked at the issue that caused him to go into battle. He asked himself if it was a worthy one. Then he looked at the nature of his life and the nature of the life of his enemy. He asked himself if he could honour that life through fighting. He asked himself if he was prepared to continue his spirit journey in another form over the issue. When he was satisfied that it was a righteous and honourable way, he continued.

"But most importantly he thought about the foe. He thought about the foe being a man not unlike himself, with

FIND AN
*insight*
THAT HEALS

a family, loved ones, a tribe, a community. He thought about how all those things shaped his own life and how much he loved being a part of that vital energy. He thought about how his people would feel if he were to be taken away on the battlefield. When he found an emotional harmony with his foe he offered a prayer for him and his people. He prayed for their well-being, for their prosperity, for their happiness. He prayed for their future.

"When he had done these things and the idea of going into battle was still as strong, he said to himself, "If I can pray for my enemy and want those things for him that I want for myself, if I can consider him as a sacred part of Creation like myself, then I can go to battle and risk my life, because if I can do all those things, then today is a good day to die. Those are the things he considered in a prayerful way. If, in the end, he could not bring himself to pray for his foe and for the well-being of his foe's people, he would not allow himself to fight.

"So when you repeat those words, know that they are spiritual words. They are not militant, angry, vengeful words. Nor are they prideful. They are the words of one who has reflected on the sanctity of life. They are the words of one who has considered harmony and the honouring of a spiritual way. So in the end, they are the words of a very brave person, because only when you can face the foe with integrity are you truly brave."

That's what he told me. He was a very wise man.

Unfortunately, the amount of fear I carried and the false

pride resulting from that fear did not allow me to fully understand what he meant. It would be years before I really got it. I spent a long time on a merry-go-round of drunkenness. I drank because I could not defeat the foe in me. I could not best the belief that I was inherently invaluable, that I was not worthy, that I did not deserve good things and happiness. Those beliefs were at the core of my being and I only ever knew how to fight them with drink, to drown them, to wash them away momentarily. When I awoke, as I always did, I awoke with shame and guilt and more fear. I did not know then that fear and courage share a common trait: they both perpetuate themselves. The difference is that courage is spiritual energy and fear is a spiritual lack. Courage is humility in action and fear is the belief in separateness in action. As long as I reacted with the fear in me, I could not face the foe with integrity, and without integrity all battles are fought with ego and pride and fear itself. That is the opposite of the warrior way as Crazy Horse lived it. And that is the essence of what Albert Lightning was telling me in that story that night.

The stories of my people are invasive. They sit in your consciousness after you hear them and they begin to sprout and grow despite your inability to grasp their full meaning. That's what makes them so powerful. They inhabit you. As time goes by, if you allow it, they become you. That's what happened to me. Eventually, I found another Teacher who was able to help me explore the dark channels of my unfounded belief in my unworthiness. She was a therapist. She guided me back to the days of my childhood when trauma had been introduced into my life and I had learned the primal nature of fear. Together we learned how I had become emotionally crippled, how abuse had formed the wounded psyche and the wounded spirit I carried throughout my life. She was not an Indigenous woman. She did not need to be. She was simply a caring, compassionate human being with insight. A seer, or as it is said in our circles, a see-er. She saw me in my disconnectedness and she helped me reconnect. She plugged me in to the energy of things. She taught me that I had the strength to move beyond those initial primal wounds if I would allow myself to work at it. I did, and I healed. I did the work with the focused belief that I never needed to qualify, to become worthy. I did it with the belief that I had always been worthy, that I came here worthy and that I was born out of humility as a sacred part of everything. I did the work out of bravery and I found my way to faith.

There's a funny part to that. See, when I was young and confused, when I was operating with an adopted anger, people would always tell me, "Richard, you have to have faith." That always irritated me. For the most part I didn't know what to have faith in. Added to that was my misconception that faith was a show of weakness, that having faith was the polar opposite of doing what one needed to do without advice or aid from anyone. So I made faith into an acronym. Back then when they told me I needed faith I said that *faith* stood for "find another Indian to hassle." Then, as I gradually emerged into the light of Albert Lightning's story by embracing my therapist's teaching, I discovered a new acronym. Acting with humility and courage I was able to find new and powerful ways to see the story of my life. I was able to envision my journey as filled with points of light I had never seen before. I began to allow myself to look at old hurts for the teachings they held instead of the wounds, and in this way I was able to live the words of Crazy Horse. I fought with integrity and each time I did I found another insight that healed me. I moved further into the light of my reality: that I had always been a spiritual being borne on the Sacred Breath of Creation, never separate, never disconnected, never discarded. Every time I fought the foe that way I found the acronym I use today. *Faith* has come to mean "find an insight that heals."

The spiritual byproduct of courage is faith. We only come to be brave with humility as our guide. We only find humility by coming to believe in the spiritual truth that we are borne on the Sacred Breath of Creation, and that because of that truth we are a Sacred part of everything. It is a circle. It is complete—and one cannot function without the other, in incompleteness.

To live with courage is to face the foe with integrity. Our species has a common foe regardless of our cultural background. That foe is fear, and it brings us to our third ceremony.

WE ARE
*a sacred part of*
CREATION

## THE THIRD CEREMONY:
# The Vision Quest

WE ARE A sacred part of Creation. This is truth. This is
spiritual. However, as soon as we begin our Earth Walk we
learn the opposite. We learn separation. We learn the fear
of disconnecting from the shelter of our mother's belly, and
because fear perpetuates itself it leads to more fear. Fear of
hunger. Fear of abandonment. We learn to cry out for comfort,
for reassurance, for our needs to be met, and that keening
continues for most of our lives until we rediscover harmony
and connectedness, and learn that separation is a myth and an
ungrounded fear.

The fear of separation is powerful. It's primal and it
operates in our lives unseen and secretive, only making itself
known when we become brave enough to look for it. Some
of us are fortunate enough to have loving, nurturing families
and our journey is marked by their presence. Some of us
have strong religious affiliations that enhance the meaning
of our lives. Still others find soulmates who grace us with
the depth of their love. But within all of that—because we
are a human family and we are all born gasping for the same
breath—resides the pulse of original fear. Separateness. It is
our common cry.

We learn fear. We become afraid of the dark. We become
afraid to be alone. We learn to fear injury. We learn to fear

death. All of that can be traced back to the original fear of separation. But if we can learn the teaching of Humility and learn to act with Courage and to engender Faith, we can unchain ourselves from the shackles of our fears. All it takes is Allowing.

This ceremony is all about Allowing ourselves to be brave. It asks us to step beyond what we have come to accept as security in the world. It asks us to move out of our comfort zone. It asks us to return to the state of innocence that we were born in and to embrace it despite ourselves. It has been called many names in the reinterpretation process that labels most things. Mostly it has been called a Vision Quest and has been greatly romanticized. It has come to mean a Technicolor visit with the spiritual realm, complete with visitations from ancient guides and animal Teachers and sweeping vistas of prophetic energy. It has sold a lot of books and movies and it has made a lot of false teachers a great deal of money. It has led to a perception of tremendous mystery and sanctity. It has led to my own people refusing to share it with those from other cultures for fear of it being taken away. But it is spiritual and belongs to all of us because we are all spiritual beings. And once we remove the romantic notion of hallucinatory, spectral waking dreams, it becomes a process of remembering. That's all. Remembering.

See, we've forgotten that we are a sacred part of everything. The grievous state of the planet these days is evidence of that. We've forgotten that we actually live on a planet just as we've forgotten that the planet is our Mother, that she gives us everything we need to survive. We've forgotten our original instructions to walk gently. A Vision Quest is a ceremony that allows us to allow ourselves to remember that. The vision we are ultimately granted is of our connectedness, our relationship, our kinship to everything. When we remember this oneness we move closer to the fullest possible expression of ourselves, and the sacred Medicine of that journey is the act of remembering itself.

Traditionally, a Vision Quest takes four days and requires a traditional teacher to act as a guide, to interpret protocols and act as a prayerful intermediary. But this one, this simplified and doable ceremony, takes a single day. It can be done by anyone from any culture who seeks to rediscover and remember their place in the scheme of things, who seeks to forgo their sense of lostness and separation for a vision of belonging and kinship and harmony with the planet. It is for anyone who craves spirituality and a spiritual way. It is for the human family.

All ceremony begins with preparation. Preparation is the foundation upon which the ceremony is built and in this case you begin days before. Find a place on the land that is away from things. It might be a hilltop. It could be the shore of a lake or a river. It might be a glade in a forest or a rock ledge or a fallen log in a clearing. Take the time to take yourself to the land and find a place that resonates for you, feels special, calm, peaceful, filled with spirit. It may take you some time to find this place, but the search is a crucial part of the journey. To find the right place, you sacrifice time, energy, money and pride. Perhaps you need to ask someone for permission to go there. That's another sacrifice: having the humility to ask. When you find this place, offer some tobacco or another gift from your culture along with a prayer of thankfulness for the gift of this place of connection. Go there a few times on your own and sit quietly. Do nothing else but sit there and be.

When you choose a day for this ceremony, make sure to clear your schedule completely for a period of twenty-four hours. You will be occupied from one morning to the next. Take care of your responsibilities to ensure that nothing conflicts with this spiritual time. When you have the day set you can begin the rest of the preparations.

The day before, begin by telling yourself that you are embarking on a valuable part of your Earth Walk. Concentrate on every part of the preparations in this way. Focus your mental energy on the task. Allow nothing else to crowd your thinking. Focus and begin with the Sacred Breath ritual. Take time to ensure that you feel your spirit moving. Take time to inhabit that ritual completely. When you feel that connection you can begin the rest of the preparatory work.

With your mind focused on your desire to grow and learn, take yourself to the market or the grocery store. Choose your favourite foods that you can prepare ahead of time. As you pick these items, think of Mother Earth and her generosity. Think of the rains that nurtured this food. Think of the trees that breathed to create the rain. Think of the winds that shook the leaves of those trees. Think of the sky that held the wind. Think of the planet whose atmosphere contains the sky. Think of the universe that cradles the planet. In this way, you gather your food in a spiritual manner and your thinking becomes a circle. It becomes spiritual.

Return home and prepare a meal with your gathered items. Place your meal in the refrigerator for after the ceremony and offer a prayer of thanks for the gift of it.

On the morning of the ceremony, set your alarm clock to wake you as close to sunrise as possible. If you need to sleep alone so you do not disturb your family, make this sacrifice as well. When you awake go someplace quiet and do the Sacred Breath ritual. Take the time to inhabit the process, to feel your breathing and your energy. When you are satisfied, have a good breakfast and enjoy the taste of the food. It will be the last food you eat for twenty-four hours.

Once you have eaten, take a blanket, some water, a warm jacket or sweater—or clothing that suits the season—and put it all in a pack along with a pencil and a notebook. Then, once you are ready, travel to the special place on the land that you have chosen. Focus on the idea that you are embarking on a very special ceremony. Think of nothing else. When you arrive there find a comfortable place to sit, put your water nearby, sit on your blanket and allow yourself to do the Sacred Breath ritual again. Maintain it for as long as you can. Try to feel this special place you have chosen. Try to feel its energy all around you. When you feel that, open your eyes. Say a prayer, offer a spiritual gift and relax.

Your mission is to stay there, in that spot, for the course of that whole day and the following night. Drink only when you absolutely have to. Concentrate on using your senses to come into the flow of energy in the place you've chosen. Look at things. Look intently and mindfully and write notes about what you see in your notebook. Look at how shadows play. Look at textures. Look at motion. Write down how looking at the world so closely makes you feel.

Practise listening. Close your eyes so you can isolate your hearing. Breathe like you do in the Sacred Breath ritual and listen mindfully. Try to hear the wind or the breeze in the trees or grasses. Work at hearing the sound of birds and the small creatures moving around you. Try to distinguish each individual sound. Open your eyes now and then and write observations down in your notebook. Write how sitting with your eyes closed listening to the world makes you feel. Don't write thoughts. Record only feelings.

Close your eyes and breathe through your nose. Try to determine how the land smells. Try to differentiate the aromas of the soil, grass, blooms and even the wind. Focus your attention solely on your sense of smell and try to isolate particular odours from others. Open your eyes and record your observations. Write down any strong feelings that come.

Walk slowly and gently around the small area where you were seated. Pick things up. Run your hands over them or rub them on your skin. Pick up stones, twigs, leaves, moss, tree bark, grass. Examine everything. With a handful of such things, return to your seat, close your eyes and feel each of them. Let your fingers trace each of them while you breathe and try to see them with your touch. Write down how this makes you feel.

With your senses engaged just sit and experience this place you have chosen. Feel how your body feels while it rests there. Feel the energy of the world in that spot. Imagine yourself emitting your own vibration, sending the flow of your energy out into the great circle of energy all around you. If thoughts try to intrude use the Sacred Breath anchoring thought: "I breathe in the power of Creation." Relax. Enjoy the feeling of connection that comes.

Hunger will arise. When it does, take a drink of water. Write down how hunger makes you feel. Focus your mind on your breath again until the feeling fades, as it will with your directed thought energy. Each time it arises, repeat the same process.

Eventually evening will begin to fall and you will find yourself becoming anxious. This is natural. As a species we have lost touch with the planet. We have allowed ourselves to feel secure and safe only when there are separations between us and the natural world. As darkness falls this feeling will become more pronounced and you may feel like abandoning the ceremony. This is the time for courage. Remember how you used your senses to anchor you to this place. Remember the feelings that were engendered. Remember the peace you felt and go to it and sit with that calm energy. Remember that you are a sacred part of Creation and try to sit with that humility. By now you may be feeling hungry, alone and frightened. Your senses will be working overtime. The air is cooler and sound is amplified. You will not be able to see and this might frighten you even more, because you may imagine dangers that are not there. But remember the teaching of humility: that there is no separation, that you are a vital part of Creation. Remember that you experienced this place with your senses and feelings and that you know it well. You allowed it to become a part of you and your experience. Direct your thinking toward the idea that Mother Earth is a benign and humble being conducive to life, and that she is your home. Relax. Be brave.

As time passes you will grow accustomed to the feeling of being out on the land. Your blanket and your warm clothing will provide you with shelter. You can drink sips of water to alleviate your hunger. When there is weakness in you, sing a song or offer a prayer aloud. Try to inhabit the space you are in completely and do the Sacred Breath ritual as often as you need to in order to calm yourself and find courage. Eventually the light will begin to break in the east, you will be able to see clearly and the anxiety will fade with the dark.

When morning has fully broken and you are ready, leave a spiritual gift and a prayer of gratitude for the experience. In that prayer offer thankfulness for all the feelings you experienced and for the opportunity to sit and be with the planet in a totally unobstructed way. Give thanks for your safety. Give thanks for the hunger and discomfort. When you are finished, perform the Sacred Breath ritual again, and then get up and make your way home. Once you are back in your home slowly set out your meal. Offer thanks and eat slowly and in a spirit of celebration.

In this ceremony you have faced your foe with integrity; you have faced your fear. You have sat alone and unprotected through an entire night. You have forgone the need to eat. You have allowed yourself to be one with your surroundings and with the planet. You have been prayerful, mindful and purposeful throughout the entire process. You have exemplified courage. Praise yourself, for there are not many who would undertake such a deliberate stepping away from perceived security. After a period of rest make arrangements to share the story of your experience with friends. This is the final part of the ceremony and perhaps the most vital. Tell them everything, including what you wrote in your notebook, and focus on the feelings arising from your experience. Tell them why it was important for you to take this step. Tell them how you feel about the planet now that the ceremony is over.

Through this retelling you will garner vision. The vision you come away with will be connectedness and it is a powerful and sacred medicine. Your mission now is to reflect on that feeling and find the personal teachings that live within it and share them with others. In fact, you may pass on the process of the ceremony and find a group of people to repeat it with. This is a powerful thing. All you need to do as a group is to designate enough space for each person to be alone with the land. It might be a hundred feet. It might be a quarter mile. Whatever feels right for everybody. But there can be no talking, no communication throughout the length of the ceremony. When it is over, gather at a designated meeting place and sit and share your food and your experiences with each other. Talk openly about how you faced every hardship and how you each felt alone with the planet. Talk about the feeling of pushing out the flow of your energy into the flow of the energy of the planet. In this way you will remember and the gift of vision, of seeing yourself as a sacred part of everything, will be complete.

*peace*
IS THE
REASON
I GO TO
COMMUNE WITH
*Mother Earth*
AND
*peace*
IS THE
GIFT
I AM OFFERED IN
RETURN

WHEN I PERFORMED this ceremony for the first time I was terrified. When I was a toddler I was subjected to abuse. My Native family lived in the bush and we kids were sometimes forced to hide from the adults in the bush at night. Those events and those nights in the bush caused great trauma to live in me and as a child I was always afraid of the dark. Terrified. The ghosts of those events haunted me and because my abuse happened in darkness, the residual trauma was elevated when I was alone at night. It abated some as I grew older but never completely went away. It was even more severe if I was alone in the bush at night. I could never explain why such absolute terror rose in me. It was very confusing because I am Ojibway, a member of a tribal culture in which life was framed by a bush experience, and I felt a deep sense of cultural shame that I never spoke to anyone about. As an adult it was all I could do to force myself to try to sleep in a tent. Every sound in the night made me start and the dislocated feeling would envelop me and I would be in terror again. I did not understand the nature of my trauma then and I did not understand my reactions to dark nights in the bush.

So when I began to take the steps I'm sharing with you now and it came time to assert bravery and be alone on the land in the darkness, the terror was so intense I thought I would bolt. But I had a very gentle teacher in Jack Kakakaway. Without knowing the specifics of my anxiety, he understood, and he took the time to explain in very clear terms what the ceremony was about and what its practice aimed to engender in me.

"It's about vision," he said. "But not about what your eyes can see. Sometimes what we think we see is what we come to know about an experience. But our eyes can deceive us. So this vision you quest for is a spiritual vision. It's a vision that comes from experience and we only ever truly experience the world when we shut off our minds and use our senses. When we touch, taste, hear, see and intuit the world around us, and we find a peaceful, calm way to do that, we find a vision common to all of us; we see how we are a spiritual part of everything.

"If that is your aim and your desire, you can sit through fear. You can be brave and face it with integrity. You seek vision out of humility because you recognize that you do not see, that you do not know, that you do not comprehend, that you feel separate. That humility allows you the bravery, the courage to seek vision, and when it is over the spiritual gift that comes to you is a measure of faith. Faith: an unshakable belief that you are joined, protected and sacred.

"When you know yourself as sacred, when you know yourself as a spiritual part of all the great creative energy around you, and you can sit alone with it, without protection or the need for the physical things we come to believe we absolutely need to feel safe, you have found vision. You can see."

I heard his words and I understood them. I wanted to achieve what they promised. Still, that first night was intense. I was in the mountains of Alberta. Alone in a great wilderness where bears, cougars and wolves roam. I could imagine all the harm that could come to me and I allowed myself to do that for the first while. But when I focused on learning the place where I sat with the full range of my senses and then my intuition, I became so lost in the depth of that experience that I just forgot to be afraid. Just forgot. Later, when the fear triggered by darkness and night arose, I remembered and I used those tools again to centre myself in that place. The night passed before I knew it and I emerged from there capable of being alone on the land in dark or in light.

These days I choose to be alone. When I walk in the mountains behind my home I still use all my senses to experience my surroundings and I am never afraid, never anxious, never a victim of my trauma. Instead, I find a union, a harmony, a joining with everything around me and it gives me peace. Peace is the reason I go to commune with Mother Earth and peace is the gift I am offered in return. Peace too, you see, perpetuates itself.

Of all the things that come from this process, perhaps the greatest is the ability to determine how little we actually need to survive. Through forsaking food and feeling the bite of hunger, assuaging it with water and patience, we see how controlled we are by the need to consume. This ceremony shows us that we actually need very little to flourish and that the planet can support us all. There always was and there always will be enough if we return to and obey the original instructions— walk gently upon the Earth and do each other no harm.

One of the greatest fears we carry as a species is the fear of lack, of not having enough. Many people who were adults as I was growing up had lived through the Great Depression of the 1930s. That experience instilled in them the lurking fear of lack and hunger. What this fear engendered in return was a need to work hard and to deliberately stave off that eventuality. When you are always afraid that there will never be enough you act out of fearful energy and there can be no harmony. The fact that there are hundreds of millions of people in our world who chronically do not have enough to eat is testimony to the presence of disharmony. People fear. When that energy is pervasive, people suffer. We become so attached to protecting and enhancing our own little corner of the world that we allow ourselves to forget that we are all connected, that we are all part of creative energy and that everything we do or choose affects someone or something else. That's just how it works. So when we fear lack, we create it. Maybe not in our own lives but certainly in the lives of others somewhere on the planet. If fear perpetuates itself then fearful energy perpetuates itself as well, and fearful energy creates disharmony.

But when you sit out on the land alone and without anything you quickly come to see how little it actually takes to get by. The Earth is a tremendous teacher and by taking the time to sit with her, to sense her and to intuit the implications of aloneness is to be granted a vision of the Earth, and what is required for her survival, that is unsurpassed. My people understood this when they created the ceremony that has come to be called the Vision Quest. They understood that only through an intimate understanding of the Seven Grandfather Teachings could one hope to journey well through life and that it was vital to be able to experience the world in its fullness before that could happen. They also understood that spiritual energy is the specific energy in which everything is present and nothing is present all at the same time. An empty mind is a full mind. A human being has to have nothing to have everything. That was the reason why we were sent out without possessions or anything that had come to represent safety and security. Traditional Vision Quest ceremonies take place over four days and four nights and there are strict protocols that need to be followed with the guidance of a traditional teacher, elder or shaman. Participants stay alone all that time, though the guide might check in on them silently now and then. The point is to meet the world in openness and solitude and to be granted a personal vision of our place in the great circle of creative energy that is around us and inside of us always.

However, things change. Nowadays there are businesses that charge a great deal of money to take groups of tourists out onto the land on what they market as Vision Quests. Organizers provide tents and sleeping bags or other comforts and participants are never truly alone. While there may be some benefit from being part of a community that is searching for a spiritual way, these pricey ventures do not ask a sacrifice of the participants. Sacrifice is a spiritual principle and when we sacrifice our security we exemplify courage. Going out as a group does not allow us to sacrifice anything. The manifestation of faith, the spiritual byproduct of courage, is absent and the activity does not become a ceremony. It's just an outing.

See, a ceremony is a ritual that is meant to enhance our lives. It is a practice that takes us within ourselves so that upon its completion we may act outwardly different. In that it is a circle. Going inward to affect the outward. When a person practises the intent of a completed ceremony in the day-to-day circles of influence they move through, the reverse flow of energy happens. They act outwardly and it affects their inner life. This is the great spiritual intent of ceremony and the Seven Grandfather Teachings. This is spiritual. This is truth. This is Indian. This also brings us to the fourth ceremony.

## THE FOURTH CEREMONY:
# Acting Outwardly

ACTING OUTWARDLY FOLLOWS the Vision Quest
ceremony. It is ongoing and it is meant to become the basis
of living a good life. Essentially, when you experience the
world sensually instead of with the mind you are granted
vision. Then, when you step back into the world where you
live your everyday life there needs to be a continuation in
order to honour that ceremonial time. To honour, in the
Indian way, means to recognize and affirm. So the intent
of acting outwardly continues down the path started in the
Vision Quest, to hone that vision, to see even more clearly the
vibrant thread that connects us to everyone and everything.

We have now seen how little we need to survive. By
removing ourselves from the things we come to lean on for
security in our lives we realize that, as beings of spiritual
energy in constant contact with the flow of energy that is the
universe, we are never separate, never insecure or unsecured.
This is a magnificent form of enlightenment and should be
celebrated. This fourth ceremony is that celebration.

When we think of sacrifice we tend to regard it as an
archaic practice, something biblical, perhaps something
mythological. But the truth is that we make sacrifices every
waking day of our lives. It's an essential part of existence

and transformation. We just don't always recognize sacrifice for what it is. So even at our most down times, even during our periods of flagging energy, we are making sacrifices and exemplifying courage. Even if we don't know it. Especially when we don't know it.

The purpose of this ceremony is to make ourselves aware of the sacrifice and the bravery in our lives. Its intent is to allow us the spiritual energy of Choice: choosing to act as brave beings. From that singular choice comes the energy that can transform the planet.

It's all about need. Look around your home and make a list of all the things you need. Write a list as you move through your home. Do it mindfully, like all your preparations for these small ceremonies. Allow yourself no distractions. The list can be as long or as short as it needs to be, provided it is honest and complete. When it is finished compare it to the notes you made on the Vision Quest. Remind yourself of the things you wrote about your experiences sensing the Earth. Now, go back over your list of needs and ask yourself again what it is that you *truly and absolutely* need. The changes on the list will dictate your mission. What remains there, what you need to be happy and secure, will become the nature of your sacrifice.

For instance, if food is an item remaining on your list, as it likely is, your mission could be to buy a shopping cart full of food and donate it to a local food bank. Do it ceremonially.

Do it mindfully. Think about your sacrifice as you make your way to the grocery store. Think about why it is important for you to do this thing. Think about the spiritual energy you are pushing outward. Think about the effect your choice is having on people and, ultimately, on the planet.

Similarly, if clothing remains on your list, find a meaningful way to donate clothing. Whatever exists as a need on your list dictates your mission to give that item back to the planet because in truth, that is exactly where it came from. You know this from experience now. As time goes by, continue to honour the depth of that experience by going down your list, offering things back to the source and taking care of others in the process. It is important to allow the continuation of the circle of experience you have begun to live because when you choose to do that, when you allow yourself to live outwardly what you have experienced inwardly, there is harmony— within yourself and on the planet. You become an agent of harmony. You become an agent of change.

Some things will be bigger and harder and the sacrifice you are asked to make will be greater but that is the nature of life. Embrace it. Eventually you will come to see that your fear of lack, of never having enough, will fade. You will be freed.

In traditional tribal times when hunters returned with game, the very first thing they did was make sure that everyone else in the community had food first. They walked from wigwam to wigwam and offered meat to each family. Then they took what was left for themselves. In our world today we do the opposite. We take for ourselves first and then maybe we get around to thinking of others. This ceremony asks us to return to a tribal mindset, to remember that we are all related, we are all kin and that we need each other. Following that teaching is a spiritual act. The principle of courage is exemplified by our choice to allow ourselves to sacrifice. It is tribal. It is the essence of us, regardless of our cultural background, because we are all tribal people. Remembering that is the great gift of this fourth ceremony.

When Ernestina sacrificed her vision so that Bison could go on to help the People, anonymous beings she had no knowledge of, she set spiritual energy in motion. She became transformed. In our world today, such transformation is possible when we allow the act of sacrifice to take place in our lives.

Everyone has a Magic Mountain, something that we desire so deeply to see in our lives that it drives us forward. Everyone has to take the risk of going beyond our safety zones, our known territories, in order to find those beings that are there to help us. Our Frog, Horse and Coyote. We all need to use our senses to experience the world and when we do we are able to go beyond our own needs and help others. When we do that we are granted vision on a scale that transforms us. That is the blessing in this fourth ceremony.

Still, it is a difficult part of the journey. It's made onerous by our ingrained fears of lack and failure. The fear of not having enough drives us to hoard, to overspend and to protect those things we deem important to our security. The fear of failure drives us to overwork and to commit ourselves to disciplines that eliminate spiritual activities like play, or sharing stories with one's community. In a fast-paced world, being brave takes a back seat to getting, gaining, having. But the truth is that being brave is the one simple spiritual act that allows all of those things to happen. Choosing to act with courage is the doorway to spiritual transformation. However, the nature of our lives makes it a difficult thing to do.

When we begin to live by the principles we find in these small, doable ceremonies, an extraordinary thing happens. The very act of living as a tribal person, as someone connected to every other being and every other thing on the planet, makes our life itself a ceremony—a ceremony that elevates us and enhances us, makes us more, gets us closer to our highest possible expression of who we were created to be. That is the ultimate goal of living with the Seven Grandfather Teachings.

*Choosing to*
ACT WITH COURAGE
*is the doorway*
TO SPIRITUAL
TRANSFORMATION

WHEN YOU MEET someone whose spiritual journey has become central to their vision of themselves, it's wonderful. Spiritually centred people have calmness, a placid nature you can feel standing at their side, and they radiate a sense of rootedness that's magnetic to those of us still footloose and wandering. My tribal teachers were all like that, especially Jack Kakakaway. He lounged. Even in moments of preparation or hurry to get things done on time, he still oozed a casual, slouching nonchalance that was wonderful to see. Nothing seemed to be able to pierce that effortless calm. When he offered teachings to me they were always given with that laid-back, laconic ease, and because of that they came to resonate within me. They always felt like stories.

Once we were walking in the bush. It was a perfect cloudless day in the mountains of Kananaskis Country, outside of Calgary. The air barely moved and we could smell and hear everything around us. When we entered a glade I looked up and saw a golden eagle soaring over us. I stopped and watched the great bird as it held its wings motionless and skimmed the treetops and ridges. It was beautiful.

"That's how I want to be," I said. "Moving through my life as gracefully as that."

Jack didn't speak for a while. We walked and every now and then I got another glimpse of the eagle through the tops of the trees. "Not so easy as it looks from down here," he said. "From here it looks as though that bird has no worries, no cares— he's just a powerful being soaring over everything.

"But the truth is that it takes a heck of a lot of work to be that graceful."

He took the eagle feather from his hat brim and motioned for me to sit beside him on a log. "This feather looks like one thing at first but if you look closely at it there's a lot more there."

He traced the long stem with a finger. "On each side of this shaft there are filaments. They don't look like much all on their own but together they make up the feather. When that bird is flying she has to know how to work each one of those filaments to capture the flow of the air and direct it. There's thousands of them. Hundreds on each feather. So it takes a lot of learning to know how to do that and to approach the grace you envy.

"Then there's the wind. When the eagle's up there so high she's got to learn how to read the treetops and the clouds and the far horizons so that she knows the state of the wind. Takes keen vision. She needs to be able to look at the grasses and see the effect of the wind on them. She needs to be able to feel updrafts and low-pressure areas and know what they mean to her flight. She needs all of this knowledge to approach the grace you crave.

"She's born with the dream of flight. But flight takes work. When she fledges, when she gets her feathers, she begins her education on how to use them. She flaps them awkwardly in the nest, gets used to the feel of them, the idea of them. Then on the day she leaves that nest she takes all the bravery and faith and belief in herself as a sacred creation and jumps. There's no other way to learn to fly. She just jumps.

"Oh, there's a long period of learning. There always is when you're trying to find freedom, and she has to content herself with slow, awkward flights that aren't more than a few yards long. But she gets stronger and the flights get longer and she learns more and more about how to work each of her feathers. Then one day she's higher than she's ever been and her wings are tired from carrying her so high. She looks down and sees the world far below her and as magnificent as it is, she's scared. She wants to rest but she's incredibly high. She has seen other eagles soar. She's seen them with their wings held out proudly, cutting huge circles in the sky. So she gathers her courage and she holds her own wings out just like they did.

"She wobbles at first but once she sees that she won't fall she starts to use her knowledge of herself, starts to manipulate each filament in each feather to direct the air through her wings to hold her in position. It takes time and it takes dedication but she learns, and eventually it comes automatically because she's in touch with her identity.

"That's how much work it takes to soar so gracefully. We admire it because it looks so effortless. But it takes incredible perseverance. It takes humility. It takes courage. It takes faith. But those things too become automatic when you choose them enough. When you choose them enough you get in touch with your identity too. But it takes work and perseverance to get there."

Later he explained how the feather is a symbol of the journey we are on as human beings. The feather's shaft is the spiritual way we all want to travel. It is laid out according to spiritual principles. Each of the filaments he pointed out earlier is a choice that our lives ask us to make along the way. Every choice has the ability to take us from the path but it is also the way back at the same time.

"Choice is like that," he said. "It creates itself over and over. You are always free to just choose again. Just choose to walk back to the path."

There are two sides to an eagle feather. The one side represents good-minded choices and the other represents their opposite. "It's about balance," he explained. "Choice is a powerful teacher and Creator allowed us the freedom to make our own on the way to discovering ourselves. But each choice carries within it the power to choose again, and out of the mindful act of choosing to work our way back to the path comes the vision of who we were created to be. Our identity. When you make a choice that leads you astray but choose again in order to return to the path, that is an act of bravery, an act of faith, and this is why an eagle feather is such a sacred gift.

"We give eagle feathers to symbolize the courage we see each time we see an eagle soar across the sky. The courage that comes from being committed, perseverant, and believing in Creator's course. The courage to move beyond doubt and to gain knowledge. The courage to find balance in our lives. That's what the eagle and the feather represent to us."

Every choice HAS THE *ability* TO TAKE US FROM the path

but IT IS ALSO the way back AT THE same time

Again, it took me years to fully assimilate what he taught me that day. In my own way I had to first learn to make short awkward flights too. But these days I find that I have the ability to soar. Not always. Sometimes I choose something that leads me to stray from the path and I struggle and have to choose again to return to it. But the teaching of the feather tells me that it takes such bravery to find balance, to learn more of the man that I am, to touch my identity. There are no right or wrong choices because there is no judgment from a loving Creator. There are only stronger or weaker choices. We find ourselves through the power of choice, and courage is the principle that allows us to continue to choose when we find ourselves straying from the spiritual path. Each filament of our lives plays a necessary part in our soaring.

# MINWAADENDAMOWIN:
## respect

**Rueben was** an inquisitive raven. Of course, all ravens are inquisitive, but Rueben was a notch above even the most curious bird. The talk in the forest was that Rueben was nosy. Prying, even. Downright intrusive sometimes. The fact was that Rueben was in a constant state of amazement at the world. His beady black eyes gleamed and glittered in excitement whenever he flew off from his favourite perch in the forest. There was a gold mine of fascinating and wondrous things to see and investigate. Normally ravens are drawn to shiny things and even though Rueben shared that fascination with his friends and cousins, his curiosity went even further than that. Rueben wanted to see and experience *everything*.

There were numerous stories in the forest about Rueben's rampant curiosity. Squirrels told of his glossy black head suddenly poking into their nest holes high in the trunks of trees just to see the freshly born babies his sharp ears could hear mewling and squealing. Beavers spoke of how he would make suggestions about the particular design of a new dam after watching them build dozens of them. The bears grumbled good-naturedly about his penchant for beating them to the summer berry patches and his taste for the plumpest, juiciest berries. Or the sight of him perched on a branch above their winter dens, waiting for them to emerge, and then squawking in glee at the sight of their sleepy rumpled shapes. Even the herons told stories about Rueben's attempts to imitate their patient one-footed stance in the shallows and the laughs he drew when he attempted to spear minnows. Everyone in the forest had a story about Rueben. Everyone spoke fondly of him and even though they might have been aggravated by his hopping presence they appreciated his quest for knowledge and his determination to understand things.

"What's that? What's that?" he would squawk suddenly from a branch and the animals got used to stopping whatever they were doing and explaining the nature of their endeavours. His eyes always gleamed and he always listened respectfully. Then he would fly away to his favourite perch high atop a great pine tree. They would see him sitting there hitching his wings and twisting his head while he considered everything they had told him. Then, once he'd reached a conclusion about the new information, he would squawk loudly and excitedly in raven talk. The forest would ring with his sharp voice and everyone knew that he'd found something new and wonderful in the world.

His parents and family were amused. They shared the insatiable curiosity of all ravens but they had never taken it to the heights that Rueben had.

"Reminds me of my daddy," Grampa Raven would say. "He'd fly far and wide just to see a wonder."

"Aren't you afraid it could get him in trouble someday?" Rueben's mother asked.

"Oh, no," Grampa Raven said. "Wonder is the glue that holds everything together. It keeps you searching, eager for more. Out of wonder comes awe and out of awe comes respect and that's the most valuable gift of all."

So Rueben flew relentlessly in search of new experiences. The forest was as familiar to him as his favourite perch in the tall pine. Even when he wasn't flying off to experience something new, Rueben sat in the tree and felt the breeze on his face and dreamed of even more magnificent things elsewhere in the world. He longed to see everything.

Then one day when the sun was high in a perfect blue bowl of a sky he saw something he had never seen before. There, seemingly hung against the sky, was a dark dot. It didn't seem to move and as Rueben watched it, the dot eased across the sky as though it were floating. It sailed and then began to bank and turn in long graceful swoops that took it lower and then higher, and eventually it began to drop lower and lower until Rueben could finally make out what it was.

It was a bird. But it was a more magnificent creature than any he had ever seen. The span of its wings was enormous. As it cruised closer to him Rueben could see powerful talons tucked under its body and when it looked down at him he saw a great yellow beak and a shining white head. He heard the flap of its huge wings. Then the great bird started to climb higher and higher into the sky and Rueben watched while it began to soar in lazy circles. The soaring was mesmerizing. He couldn't believe how such a big bird could attain such grace, such effortless motion in the air. He watched it until his neck ached and the great bird soared out of view behind a ridge.

# Wonder
IS THE *glue* THAT HOLDS
*everything*
TOGETHER

When he looked around, Rueben could see all the creatures of the forest gazing upward at the spot where the bird had vanished. Everyone, it seemed, had stopped their busyness and looked at the great bird soaring across the sky. Rueben saw marmots, squirrels, raccoons and even the bears, wolves and moose staring in rapt wonder at the suddenly empty sky. He couldn't believe it. Never before had he seen the creatures of the forest so completely overwhelmed by the presence of another being. Rueben looked up at the sky again and wished for the magnificent creature to reappear. When it didn't he felt disappointed.

But the next day he was back on his perch. He sat through the long morning and halfway through the afternoon. Then, just as he was nodding off from tiredness, he saw it. The bird came out of the west and soared across the tops of the trees a quarter mile away from him. It wasn't very high and the speed of its push across the sky made Rueben gasp. This bird was an awesome being. He could feel that from where he sat. It was brown going to a dark grey and its white head seemed to gleam in the sunlight. It carved an unwavering score across the sky and when it reached the edge of a meadow it banked hard suddenly and sailed off on a hard angle in the opposite direction, climbing high into the sky. Rueben watched as it reached its crest and set its wings and hung in the sky like the dot he had seen the day before. It was an amazing sight. Again he noticed other forest creatures staring up at it in awe.

Rueben looked up every day after that hoping to catch sight of the great bird. He asked his grandfather about it and the old raven squawked impressively. "That is Migizi, the eagle," Grampa Raven said. "She is a great being blessed with many gifts."

Rueben wanted to ask him to explain the nature of Migizi's gifts but his curiosity prompted him to find out for himself. So he returned day after day to watch the bird in flight.

He loved to watch her soar. There would always be a little catch at the back of his throat when the bird held her wings motionless in the sky. He breathed shallowly and his beak hung open in admiration. He never fluffed his feathers. Instead he stared intently at the sight of that huge bird suspended against the clear blue of the sky. Within him Rueben felt the wish to soar building. He felt a keen desire cutting through everything he knew of himself as a raven, and he wanted more than anything to be able to soar like Migizi. He wanted others to stop what they were doing and watch him as he streamed across the top of the forest. He wanted to feel the absolute freedom that he imagined soaring would give him. He wanted to emulate the great eagle. He wanted to feel like a magical creation and be respected for the quiet power he displayed.

When he thought that way he began to look at himself. His wings were coal black and despite a deep lustre that shone blue in the sun sometimes, his feathers were short and blunt and not made for graceful banks and swoops through the clouds.

His beak was straight with clumps of feathers at its underside. His feet were splayed and thin. He knew from looking at other ravens that his eyes were dark and that he blinked a lot and he could never hold the intent, grave gaze of Migizi. No, compared to that great bird Rueben was short and blunt and black, hardly a formidable or fascinating sight. Hardly a being that could draw fascination from others. Respect. Awe. Outright admiration.

But if he could soar, perhaps there was a way to create those feelings in others. If he could hold his wings motionless in the sky and hang suspended above them all they would respect him. If he could soar like Migizi maybe others would regard him like her. Surely there couldn't be all that much of a trick to it. After all, they were both birds with wings and feathers. Surely with a little pluck and practice a raven could soar like an eagle. Surely there was a place in the scheme of things for an inauspicious raven to become a magnificent being too.

So Rueben began to learn to soar.

Every day he rose extra early and flapped his way to a place in the forest where few other creatures went. There were tall trees there and vertiginous cliffs and a wide valley shaped by the cut of a river. He imagined himself launching from the cliff and soaring across the water. He envisioned jumping from the point of a tree and flapping high into the air and cutting wide, motionless glides with that landscape tilting under his wings. He imagined the feel of the wind through his feathers. He saw himself as a hard black dot against the sky dropping lower and lower in lazy circles, only to flap off in another climb into the face of the sky. He craved the sensation of becoming more: bigger somehow, more beautiful, less a raven and more revered and respected like an eagle, through the singular act of soaring.

He sat on his perch and waited. He had to calm the pounding of his heart and it took some patience to accomplish that. He was going where no other raven had ever gone. He was attempting something that none before him had ever tried. The possibility of becoming something great excited him and he had to focus very hard to settle himself. Eventually, he would calm. Then he would consider what he wanted to do. He'd seen Migizi enough times to have a rough idea how he should use his wings. He'd watched carefully and knew that the secret lay in stillness, in fearlessly holding his wings out steady no matter what the air around him was doing.

At first he leaped from the top of a pine tree and tried to soar across to the next one. This was a matter of a few feet of space and it didn't take much to accomplish it. Still, the feeling of consciously flying without flapping was sensational. He chose longer flights. He practised leaping from his perch and soaring to the ground. On these flights he could see the earth hurtling to meet him and it was all he could do to steel himself and coast downward and tilt his wings at the last moment to bring himself to a light two-footed landing. The thrill of that was exhilarating. When he found he could do it without hesitation he started to look at bigger challenges.

Rueben began to choose distances that scared him. He chose to soar over three trees, then four, then five. Soon he could pick a treetop fifty yards away and push off and soar to it. The feeling was incredible. He'd sit in the new perch and fluff his feathers and squawk his excitement and prepare himself for another foray across space.

Then he took to the cliffs. He'd been practising for a number of weeks when he chose this new and dangerous level. His wings felt stronger. He was more confident. But when he flapped his way to the edge of a cliff and sat and stared down, he was suddenly more nervous than he'd ever felt in his life. Never had he been up so high. The trees looked small and very far away. The river was a metallic ribbon. The sky felt as though it enveloped him and all around him he could feel the great empty bowl of it. This was truly the domain of eagles. It took forever, it seemed, for his nerves to settle and for the knot of anxiety in his belly to ease off.

He stared at the forest far below and chose a nice big pine tree. The distance would be greater than he'd ever soared. But he took the time to analyze how he would manoeuvre. He used his mind's eye to envision the path he would take through the air, how he would bank slightly, use the push of the breeze to his advantage, how he would use his wings at the last to set himself down at the apex of the big pine. Then he pushed off.

At first his fear controlled him. Then he resolutely set his wings and braced them against the flow of air. He hurtled across space. The angle from the cliff to the tree was steep and he gained speed quickly. He remembered to bank and he tilted his wings and felt them catch the air and he turned and the sweep of the land beneath him was magical. Rueben held his wings at the same angle and he could feel himself turn in the sky. He banked. He streamed over the top of the forest and the river valley and he wanted to screech at the sheer joy of it. Instead, he focused on the feeling of soaring and he held the bank for as long as he could. He used the cliff as a focal point and found the pine he'd chosen. He circled. He slowed. When he flapped his wings to bring himself to a halt on the topmost branch of that big pine he bobbed and swayed as his weight settled and there was a rush in his head and his heart that he was barely able to contain. Rueben had soared. He'd climbed higher than any raven ever had and jumped into space and held the air with his wings and cut a motionless swath through the sky. He had soared like Migizi. His chest filled with pride and he wanted to cry in celebration. He wanted to fly home and sit on his favourite perch and squawk his joy to his fellow creatures.

But there was more to learn. So he continued to rise early and flap off to his practice site. Every day he would climb higher into the sky. Every day he would challenge himself to rise farther up and away from the land and soar down in long elegant circles. His wings grew hardy. He grew used to the thinner air at the top of his climbs. His sense of fear lessened and he became confident in his newfound ability. When he sat

in the trees after, he would close his eyes and breathe deeply and see himself as a magnificent creation, a tremendous bird, an exemplary raven and one destined to be remembered and respected forever like the great Migizi herself.

Then, one day when he had flown higher than ever, Rueben decided that it was time to show off his new skill to his family and the creatures of the forest. It was time to unveil a great new being.

He sat at the top of his favourite pine tree and squawked in excitement. He squawked and squawked and finally creatures began to gather at the base of the tree to find out what he was so excited about. When his family was all there and a goodly sized contingent of other creatures, Rueben fluffed his feathers and shook his head and bobbed on the top branch.

"What's the fuss, grandson?" Grampa Raven asked.

"I'm going to show you something magical," Rueben said.

"What's that? What's that?" the forest creatures said in excitement.

"I'm going to show you how great a raven can be," Rueben said. "Watch me."

With that he flapped off across the trees and began to climb into the sky. He flapped in a great circle and when he reached a point that the others knew was a tremendous height he could hear them gasp. He climbed even higher. Soon the forest had become a pocked green mat and he could not make out the shapes of his family and friends. Instead there was just him and the sky. He was up so high he could see the curved rim of the world far off in the distance. He was up so high he had to fight to draw enough air to sustain him. He was in the domain of the eagles and when he ceased flapping and held out his wings to catch the air he knew that all the creatures below were staring upward in awe. Rueben raised his head and stared straight ahead. He held his wings out solidly and felt the air move under them. He banked and began a long, slow downward spiral.

It felt wonderful. He closed his eyes and allowed himself to feel the incredible freedom of soaring. He banked more and the tilt of it increased his speed. Still, he held it and imagined how the sight of him must be affecting the others. He glided across the sky like a bullet. The land streamed below him in a blur. He was free.

But he'd never soared so far for so long. His wings began to tire. They began to feel heavy. He struggled to breathe. When he tried to ease the angle of the bank he wavered crazily in the air and he could hear the gasp of the assembled creatures below him. Fear clutched at him. He tried to flap his wings to gain control but he was moving too fast and the spiral broke off and he began to spin. He spun faster and faster. He dropped lower. Soon he was a mass of flapping wings in an uncontrolled descent and when he hit the topmost branch of his favourite pine tree it knocked the air from him. Rueben tumbled down from branch to branch and when he finally hit the ground at the base of that tree he was in severe disarray. Feathers were missing and those that remained were ruffled and torn and he felt bruises all over his body. He was stunned and the earth spun. He closed his eyes and the sensation of spinning continued. He could hear the worried chatter of his friends and family. When he finally felt well enough to open his eyes he was staring into the face of Grampa Raven.

"Grandson," the old bird said. "That was the most amazing thing I have ever seen."

"Really?" Rueben croaked.

"It truly was. I've never seen anyone plummet before."

"I was soaring," Rueben said weakly.

"I think most of us will only ever recall the plummet."

Rueben moaned. "I wanted to show you all that I could soar like Migizi."

"Now why would you want to do something like that?" Grampa Raven asked.

"Because everyone stops whatever they're doing and just watches her when she soars. Everyone is silent and filled with wonder. Everyone respects her. I wanted them to respect me. I wanted them to see that I had special gifts too."

"Oh, I see," Grampa Raven said and helped Rueben to his feet. He was woozy and they hopped gingerly to a small hillock where Rueben plopped down on his belly and fluffed his feathers. "Don't you think that Migizi has respect for you?"

"How could she?" Rueben asked. "My wings are stubby and my feathers are black. I have no great strength and I don't carry a beautiful song. No one notices me when I flit around the forest."

"Ah, but you see, one of Migizi's gifts is vision, grandson. She can see sharply a long ways off and she can see what is close to her. She is aware of you and your gifts and abilities."

"But I don't see any gifts."

"Migizi does. When she soars she sees the world. Her keen eye catches everything. She knows how powerful wonder and curiosity are. She knows how great a thing it is to be sociable, part of a community, and to take the time to investigate the things and the beings around you. She knows how special it is to be able to celebrate knowledge and to be willing to share it with all who will hear you. She sees you do all of that and she carries deep respect for you."

"She does?" Rueben was impressed.

"Yes. You don't need to spend your energy trying to be someone other than who you were created to be. You have gifts. You are beautiful. You are a raven and that makes you special."

"It does?"

"Most certainly."

"Even if I can't soar?"

"Especially because of that," Grampa Raven said softly.

"What do you mean?" Rueben asked, looking up at the old raven and blinking.

"I mean that you were created to be a part of the world. You were created to belong, to fit. When you fly around and put your beak into other creatures' lives you learn something of them and in turn, something of yourself too. In that way you find that you belong. You find that they belong. When

# YOU WERE CREATED TO *belong*

you sit in the treetops and tell everyone within earshot of your discoveries, you honour those beings you squawk about. When you can honour all Creation you have respect.

"See, respect is not something you earn, Grandson. It's something you carry. It's something you give. That's the blessing of it."

Rueben sat and considered his grandfather's words. After a while he hopped back up onto his thin feet and looked up at the sky. "You mean that I don't have to soar like Migizi to be like Migizi? If I carry respect for all of Creation I already am like her? That's what you mean, isn't it?"

"Yes," Grampa Raven said proudly.

Rueben flapped off and flew in great circles through the forest. His heart was light. From then on he continued to visit with other creatures and to study the world around him. Whenever he discovered something new and fascinating he sat at the top of his favourite pine tree and proclaimed it loudly in his scratchiest raven voice. He never again tried to take to the highest part of the sky and soar like an eagle. But he never forgot the lesson in his adventure. So nowadays, when you see a raven fly you will see a part of Migizi in their travels. Flap, flap, soar. Flap, flap, soar.


RESPECT IS NOT something you earn. It's not something you aspire to or ask of others. It isn't your right or what you should expect of people. Respect, in the Ojibway world, is the ability to honour all of Creation. It is something that you offer and something that you carry within you. The spiritual blessing of respect is harmony and the spiritual byproduct is community. When you choose to honour all Creation and, in turn, allow yourself to express it in your actions, you live respectfully, and because all things move in a circle, you will become respected. But it starts with the giving. It starts with the recognition that all things exist on the Sacred Breath of Creation and that because of that we are all related, all kin, all essential to the ongoing energy, the eternal heartbeat, the one song on the one drum that is the story of our time here. When you choose to allow yourself to carry respect for all your relations, you choose to allow yourself to honour Creation and you allow yourself to live honourably. Once you accomplish that, your life itself will have become a ceremony—and that is the point of the Seven Grandfather Teachings.

A ceremony is energy moving toward the goal of harmony. The three principles we have looked at, Humility, Courage and Respect, have all led us to look beyond ourselves to see the nature of our essential place in the universe and our role in maintaining its balance. Respect, and living respectfully, is the act of bestowing honour on the process of living. It is the principle that makes the continuation of this great circle of Teachings possible. Without respect, without a sense of the inherent value of all things, a spiritual journey becomes a directionless wandering.

ALL THINGS *exist* ON THE SACRED BREATH OF *creation*

We take great pride in being a nomadic culture. In traditional times we followed game and food through the seasons. Our migrations took us to all parts of our tribal territories and along the way we had the opportunity to experience relationships with everything we encountered. When game was taken there were specific prayers said in gratitude for the animal's sacrifice and asking that the energy received from the food be directed toward good acts and good minds. It was important that all parts of that animal be put to use. There was nothing wasted or displayed pointlessly as a trophy. Instead, each part was used respectfully, and in this way, the animal was honoured. Similarly, when plants were gathered there were specific prayers of gratitude for the gift of their lives. This was especially true in the gathering of the sacred medicines of tobacco, sage, sweetgrass and cedar. The gathering of plants was seen as an act of taking the energy of a life, just like bringing down an animal. The teachers saw the truth of this and created prayers and rituals that would allow the people to respect the energy they took and to honour it by making a ceremony of its harvest.

When they moved from campsite to campsite it was important that they return each site to its original condition. The poles and coverings of wigwams were taken back into the forest. The stones used for firepits were carried back to the shores of lakes or rivers or returned to the place they had been found. This is the basis of respect: the belief that Mother Earth functions best when we do not alter her rhythm or breach her flow of energy and that Creation was not put into place by us, so we do not have the right to restrict it, contain it or change it. We can only learn to respect it and work to maintain its original condition. The Ojibway people learned this by living nomadically, walking the Earth, observing the universe and discovering the perpetual state of relationship they existed in. Kinship. Taking care of the family. When you can learn to see the Earth as your mother and the various energies around you as grandfathers and grandmothers, you learn to care and tend for them as though they were your blood relations.

Respect is seeing the innocence and purity in all things and choosing to allow ourselves to celebrate and honour them by returning them to their original condition.

When I returned to my people after twenty years in the foster care and adoption system, I had no idea what any of these things meant. My connection to the teachings of my ceremonial heritage had been broken completely when I was an infant, and at twenty-four I was lost both culturally and spiritually. I was ashamed that I knew nothing of my tribal ways. I was ashamed that I didn't know my language and that I had no idea of my tribal history. I was afraid that when my people discovered that I carried no sense of my own identity they would reject me, and that if that happened I would truly be alone and adrift in a world where there was no home.

For a long time I did not share these feelings with anyone. I kept them guarded. I believed they were a mark of my unworthiness and inadequacy. When I made choices, I made them out of those same fear-based reactions to the world. I did not choose out of respect because I did not know what respect was. I chose out of fear and fear is a self-perpetuating energy. So all I managed to create through my choices were more of the same feelings.

I lived this way for a long time. Even though I was learning about the culture, tradition and teachings of our spirituality, I had lived with fear all my life and its energy was the only kind I had ever learned to follow. I didn't know this. I only knew that my life was a constant mess of bad choices, mangled opportunities, broken relationships, new cities and towns, and repeatedly building a life from the ground up. I had gotten so used to this state of being that I did not expect my life to ever be any different. I used the teachings and ceremonies I was given like Band-Aids. I applied them to every hurt and expected them to magically make all the pain go away. I went to sweat lodges to make myself feel better, for instance, and when the glow of that wore off after a few days I became depressed and frustrated that the ceremony had not worked.

But our way is not like that. Ceremony and teachings do not exist to erase things. They are not sorcery or hocus-pocus. Instead, they are spiritual ways of being that ask us to sacrifice in order for their blessing energy to flow through us. Until I learned to sacrifice my fear, my feelings of shame, inadequacy and unworthiness, and until I sacrificed my pride by talking openly about these feelings, I was choosing to allow myself to block that healing flow of energy. I was choosing to allow myself to believe in my failure instead of the reality of who I was created to be. I did not understand that I came out into this reality in the original condition of innocence and humility. I did not understand that my original condition was one of ultimate worthiness. I did not understand that I had never needed to qualify for grace or belonging and that I never would need to. I didn't know that I was a sacred part of Creation and that because of that I would always be included no matter where I went.

I took my confusion to Jack Kakakaway. We sat on a ceremonial blanket with his sacred pipe between us. After he'd said a prayer he sat and regarded me calmly.

"What do you want?" he asked.

"I want to learn how to make ceremonies work for me," I said.

He smiled. "Our role is to work for ceremony," he said.

"I don't understand."

"I know," he said and smiled again.

He asked me why I came to ceremony. I told him that because I was a Native person, because I was Ojibway, it was what I was supposed to do. I told him that ceremony was how I would learn to find my way to the identity I had lost so long ago. I said that a ceremonial life was the pathway to my healing. I said that ceremony was what could save me from a life of constant disruption and dissatisfaction. I said that it would free me from my weaknesses.

all
THINGS
are a
CIRCLE

He sat quietly and considered my words. "You expect a lot," he said. Then he looked at me and I could see from his expression that he knew exactly where I was coming from and that he knew the feelings I carried within me.

"We bring ourselves to ceremony," he said. "That's the first truth. No matter where we come from or where we've been, we bring ourselves. We can't bring anything but our history, our story of our time here.

"The second truth is that that's all we've got. We travel from where we began to where we are now and that journey is all we have. Sure, we have desires, wishes and dreams for ourselves, but they all come from making that journey. Emotions too. Knowledge. Learning. They're all part of our journey and we bring all of it to ceremony and it's all we have.

"Unless we bring that story to ceremony and share it, let that energy out into the circle of ceremonial energy, nothing works. Nothing works because your pride is like a dam in a river. It halts the flow. You come to me to ask me for what I know but I want you to tell me what *you* know. You tell me what you know of ceremony, tradition and teachings. You tell me the story of your journey."

I couldn't believe what he was asking me. Sitting there with the sacred pipe between us, he was asking me to lead a ceremony. He was asking me to be the lead voice.

"I can't do that," I said.

"Why not?"

"I'm not qualified."

"Are you breathing?" he asked.

"Yes," I said.

"Then you're qualified. Bring yourself to ceremony. Tell me what you know."

I sat there feeling very uncomfortable. I sat for a long time without saying a word and he waited patiently. I thought about how I wanted so much to feel like a part of something bigger than myself. I thought of how much I wanted a feeling of belonging. I thought of the desperation I lived my life in. I thought of how inadequate I had always felt, and how unworthy.

"I don't know anything," I said. "I was taken away from my people when I was just a toddler and I haven't learned very much since I've been back."

That's what I said. He looked at me and smiled and made a circular motion with his hand to encourage me to continue. I swallowed hard and began to talk. I talked for over an hour. I spoke about foster homes and adoption. I spoke about living on the street, about going to jail, about drinking too much, about feeling rootless and afraid. I spoke about the feeling of hope that I got from being connected to the spiritual way of my people. Then I spoke about how fleeting that feeling was and how frustrated I felt. I talked about not knowing the stories and legends, of my ignorance of medicines, prayers, songs and the protocol of ceremonies that I had not attended because of my fear of the rejection that might occur when my ignorance was discovered.

When I finished he sat there nodding his head, considering my words. "You know a lot then," he said.

"What do you mean? I just told you everything I don't know."

He smiled. "We all come out onto the Earth in the same way. We all share a common beginning. We need to be taken care of. We need to be shown love. We need to be taught how to function. No matter who we become we all begin our journeys in the exact same condition. That original condition is innocence and humility.

"You've just told me what you believe you do not know. But if what you said is true, then you actually know what it is that you don't know. So, in fact, you told me what you know. All things are a circle. A circle is wholeness. So knowing and unknowing are the same energy. When you know what you do not know, you have knowledge. That is the truth of it."

# also by Richard Wagamese

*Starlight* (MCCLELLAND & STEWART, 2018)

*Embers: One Ojibway's Meditations* (DOUGLAS & MCINTYRE, 2016)

*Medicine Walk* (MCCLELLAND & STEWART, 2014)

*Him Standing* (ORCA BOOK PUBLISHERS, 2013)

*Indian Horse* (DOUGLAS & MCINTYRE, 2012)

*Runaway Dreams* (RONSDALE PRESS, 2011)

*The Next Sure Thing* (ORCA BOOK PUBLISHERS, 2011)

*One Story, One Song* (DOUGLAS & MCINTYRE, 2011)

*Ragged Company* (DOUBLEDAY, 2008)

*One Native Life* (DOUGLAS & MCINTYRE, 2008)

*Dream Wheels* (DOUBLEDAY, 2006)

*For Joshua* (DOUBLEDAY, 2002)

*A Quality of Light* (DOUBLEDAY, 1997)

*The Terrible Summer* (WARWICK, 1996)

*Keeper'n Me* (DOUBLEDAY, 1994)

# photo credits